OLD MAMMOTH

Being a first-hand account of Old Mammoth—the small village that preceded today's popular High Sierra resort in eastern California, Mammoth Lakes—and the beginnings of New Mammoth and skiing on Mammoth Mountain. A collection, also, of stories and memories from earlier times and from the boom and bust days of the Mammoth gold mines.

TEXT & HISTORIC PHOTO COLLECTION BY

ADELE REED

1982

GENNY SMITH BOOKS

PALO ALTO, CALIFORNIA

[COVER PHOTO]:
OLD MAMMOTH IN THE 1920S.
Harry W. Mendenhall Photo.

EDITED BY GENNY SMITH.

PHOTOGRAPH RESTORATION BY DOUGLAS C. GETTY.
COVER AND BOOK DESIGN BY LINDA MARCETTI.

Composed in Phototype Goudy and Phototype Americana by Jonathan Peck Typographer, Santa Cruz, California. Printed Offset by Braun-Brumfield, Inc., Ann Arbor, Michigan, on seventy pound Glatco Matte in an edition of 5,000 copies of which 1,500 are clothbound.

Library of Congress Cataloging in Publication Data.

Reed, Adele.
    Old Mammoth.

    Includes index.
       1. Mammoth Lakes (Calif.)—Social life and customs.
2. Mammoth Lakes (Calif.)—Description.   3. Reed, Adele.
I. Title.

F869.M275R43	1982	979.4'48	82-60130
ISBN 0-931378-04-4 (paper).			AACR2
ISBN 0-931378-05-2 (cloth).			

PUBLISHED BY GENNY SMITH BOOKS, PALO ALTO, CALIFORNIA.

DISTRIBUTED BY WILLIAM KAUFMANN, INC.,
95 FIRST STREET, LOS ALTOS, CALIFORNIA 94022.

FLYWHEEL, Mammoth Mining Company stamp mill, built in 1878. *Adele Reed Photo.*

ONE BY ONE THE LANDMARKS, the heritage of Mammoth's three eras, have disappeared. Not much is left of the old mining camps at the base of Red Mountain. Only traces remain of the town of Old Mammoth in the meadow and of New Mammoth on the highway. Yet tradition that has been handed down through the years by word of mouth and from memory, and bits of history not before recorded, collected from many people— these *do* remain, here brought together and here preserved.

Those of us who were privileged to know and enjoy the years of Old Mammoth can justly say, "We are glad we knew it then." We were all young as was the magnificent country we loved, and our memories remain vividly alive. My grateful appreciation to all our friends who shared their stories, adventures, and photographs and to Bill Reed, my partner. —*A. R.*

CONTENTS.

PART I.

ABOUT THE
AUTHOR &
THIS BOOK.

The large meadow area bordering Mammoth Creek is to this day known as Old Mammoth, though the small village that was there disappeared long ago. Here were the beginnings of today's High Sierra resort, Mammoth Lakes—popular in winter for Mammoth Mountain's superb ski slopes and popular in summer for camping, hiking, and fishing in the magnificent, wild back country. This is Adele Reed's story of life in Old Mammoth as she and Bill lived it, as well as her story of the prospectors, miners, merchants, and ranchers who came during the fifty years before.

The Reeds' arrival in Mammoth in 1927
came about this way . . .

OUR INITIAL TRIP TO Bishop and Mammoth Lakes was, no doubt, a counterpart of many others in the '20s. Enthusiastic letters from relatives, the Roy Boothe family, plus the promise of a healthful, dry climate and a good chance for work combined to put us on the road to a new part of the country and a new way of life. It was with some misgivings that we left Hollister, in a pretty coastal area, in April 1927. No one there was able to give any but forebodings on 'the desert.' Heat! Sandy roads! Services far apart! We felt a bit like pioneers adventuring afar.

Our 1924, 490 Chevrolet Sedan (4 cylinder job), newly overhauled and towing a luggage trailer, was heavily loaded, even to daughter's collie pup in a cage on the running board. And we were accompanied by mother and grandmother to visit in Bishop. We had convenient "button on" side curtains in case of bad weather, but had to view the countryside through blurry little isinglass windows. When not in use, they were kept in a roll under the back seat. As we neared Visalia, a loud noise in the motor upset our smug feeling, "no trouble, no strain." A burned out main bearing meant camping under a big oak tree beside the road for two days and nights.

Beyond Tehachapi lay the desert, unknown and unfamiliar. As we headed north the dire predictions did come true—rough roads, hot travel, blowouts, and never-ending miles ahead. Several things served to compensate—the far vistas, the realities of sun and space, beauty on every side. It was spring and the desert abloom. Then there were those big wooden, orange signs in the shape of a fish! They appeared continually, advertising services at the Hazard Garage in Bishop and, most important to us, indicated slowly lessening miles ahead.

Farther north the majestic beauty of the white-topped Sierra marching along on our left held our attention. As we neared Bishop the snow line had descended to the valley's floor. A superb sight! Finding the Boothes living on the old Yaney place, we set up camp in the yard. Lovely lawn and big shade trees surrounded a comfortable ranch home.

Bill was soon working as an equipment operator for the Forest Service (with Bill Brockman and John Maloney) opening roads—Rock Creek, Convict, and on up to Mammoth. At that time Pat McMurphy was District Ranger and the headquarters were in Old Mammoth, just across the bridge. A dirt road led across to the Shady Rest Cabin Tract, the campground, and the sawmill.

New Arrivals
In Mammoth, 1927.

As we moved into our mountain home in June, snow patches were just fading in the shadowed spots. The woods in Shady Rest Camp had that good, dampish earth, early spring aroma, in addition to the piney fragrance. A 16′ × 16′ army tent on a wooden frame and floor had a small cast-iron cook stove inside, which supplied heat as well as meals. The stove had four small lids and an oven just large enough to hold a pan of biscuits or corn bread. Cupboards, benches and table, beds along the rear wall, water bucket on a stand near the door with a dipper hanging above—with these we set up housekeeping. Chipmunks were chattering and flashing here and there. Pine Crows were "talking" overhead. It wasn't long until the spring migration of the thousands of wild canaries held the attention and wonder of all. They came, they stayed but a short time, filling the air with color and sweet song, then one day all were gone, who knows where.

Spare time during our first season was divided between fishing, wood gathering, and exploration of the beautiful country that was to be our home for many years. One entry in my notebook meant a rough time for awhile. "Aug. 4th, 1927—we just heard the banks have closed in Bishop!" I had only that day mailed in our paycheck!

Moving out for winter (usually to Bishop) and back in the spring became routine. The season of '28 found a new ranger at the Forest Service. Douglas Robinson was in charge, assisted by Lester Parent through summer months. Doug was liked by all, except, perhaps, the sheepherder who let his flock wander across the road to feed in the Forest Service yard one too many times. Doug did have a quick temper!

 CASA DIABLO HOT SPRINGS, its hot waters enjoyed for centuries by Paiutes, then by white men too. The road curving up the hill leads to Mammoth. The log cabin on the left probably was a Way Station on the Bishop Creek-Bodie stage line. *H. W. Mendenhall Photo.*

 MAMMOTH MOUNTAIN. Meadows along Mammoth Creek during Old Mammoth days. *Frasher Collection, Pomona Public Library.*

☞ **DESERT TRAVEL, 1927.** Driving from Tehachapi to Bishop was no fun. Rough roads, heat, blowouts—but we made it! *Nell Cox Photo.*

☞ **ADELE AND BILL REED,** late 1940s. *Howard Jones Collection.*

☞ **OUR FIRST MOUNTAIN HOME,** Shady Rest Camp, June, 1927. The smaller tent was for grandmother and our daughter. This became our way of life during many summers at Mammoth. *Adele Reed Photo.*

 LOGGING TRUCK. Relics from times past lingered for many years. This old truck may date back to the Home Lumber Co. of 1908 or possibly back to the mining days of 1878. *H. W. Mendenhall Photo.*

A DAY'S RIDE TO REDS MEADOW. Adele and Bill borrow horses for a day and ride the Fresno Flats Trail over the mountain through magnificent forest down to Reds Meadow, the San Joaquin River, and the Devils Postpile. Prospectors cabins from earlier days were still standing in the 1920s; very few can be located today. *Bill Reed Photo.*

 OLD MAMMOTH, as those who lived during Old Mammoth times will always remember it—a few scattered cabins, the huge meadow well watered, and wildflowers two feet high. *Stephen Willard Photo, probably in the 1930s.*

Willard
No. 963

PART II.

BEFORE OLD MAMMOTH: LAKE MINING DISTRICT, 1877.

Mining was the key that unlocked the treasure chest of the eastern Sierra, one of the last regions of California to be settled. Vast deserts on three sides and an immense mountain barrier on the other kept white men away until relatively late in California's history. But the discovery of the Comstock Lode's blue-black silver ore in 1858, east of Lake Tahoe, changed that overnight. A torrent of men from the played-out Mother Lode flooded east across the Sierra to the Comstock. Rumors and dreams spurred some on farther, east into the desert ranges and south along the Sierra to prospect its eastern slope. Rich gold and silver discoveries at

Aurora and Bodie, tales of lost mines, and strikes near Mill Creek (Lundy) Canyon, Mono Lake and Benton kept them searching and ever-hopeful.

One June day in 1877, four prospectors hunting for the Lost Cement Mine located the Alpha claim on Mineral Hill east of Summit Lake (Lake Mary) and organized Lake Mining District. The following year General George Dodge of Civil War and Union Pacific fame bought the Mammoth group of claims and organized the Mammoth Mining Company. News that the company was running four tunnels into Mineral Hill and constructing a tramway and 20-stamp mill, and rumor that this was the "largest bonanza outside Virginia City" sparked a short-lived rush to the Mammoth gold mines. It's said a thousand people flocked to Mammoth City the summer of 1878, and perhaps fifteen hundred the next.

INERAL HILL THEY CALLED it and plastered its reddish slopes with claims—The Mammoth, Big Bonanza, Headlight, Big Red, Monte Cristo. Mineral Hill east of Lake Mary, whose rich pockets of silver and gold led to incorporation of the Mammoth Mining Company, which in turn ignited a rush to Mammoth and wild speculation in 1878. Mineral Hill that lured those first prospectors and pioneers to climb the steep, rough road—afoot, on horseback, by wagon and team—to build three little "cities" midst the wild grandeur of an early mining district in Mono County, California.

THE MINING CAMPS:
MAMMOTH CITY, PINE CITY,
MILL CITY.

Mammoth City, the largest in Lake Mining District, sprawled across the low rocky slope opposite Red Mountain, as Mineral Hill has come to be known. Pine City, sometimes called Lake City and next in size, was built near Lake Mary in the timber. It is almost impossible now to realize that the shores of Lake Mary used to echo to the lively sounds of a booming mining town—the celebrations, the teeming life and hustle common to gold and silver camps where anticipation was in the air! As late as the '20s several fine log cabins still stood in old Pine City. Mill City was down the ravine below Mammoth City near the big Mammoth Mining Company Mill. Ore from several tunnels into the mineral mountain's steep northwest face was transported by tramway down to the mill.

Ghosts all three, these many years, and all but forgotten—these proud little "cities" wrote and lived the introductory chapter to the fabulous Mammoth Lakes we know today. The struggle to work and to live in this rugged country of high, thin air, short summers, long, cold and snowy winters, lasted but a few short years. In this time the towns were established, home, business and office. Lower, Central and Upper Mammoth Avenue, the main business street of Mammoth City, was lined with buildings. Typical boom camp architecture—rough frame buildings with false fronts, a log cabin here and there, and many dug-out type dwellings up the hillside to the north. Parts of walls and foundations beneath the brushy overgrowth indicate the style found in most old mining camps: field-rock and mortar walls, no windows, a doorway opening, the rear wall being the rocky hillside. A stove pipe projected at the rear and roofs were of boards covered with scraps of tin and earth. Home, sweet home for the courageous people gathered together far above the valleys.

WATER DIVERSIONS: DITCHES & FLUMES.

Water was essential to the three camps. Water needed to power an arrastra just below Pine City was diverted from Coldwater Creek above Lake Mary. A ditch carried it along the side of Red Mountain to a wooden flume leading to the large wooden water wheel that drove the arrastra. This arrastra was near the junction of the present Lake Mary Road and the side road to Lake Mary Store.

Water was ditched from Lake Mary downhill to Mammoth City. It continued down the draw, with a side ditch taking water easterly. This side ditch, later known as the Bodle Ditch, irrigated Windy Flat and the meadow where oxen and other stock (and later, dairy cows) grazed. The main ditch continued down to Mill City.

A little known board-covered ditch carried water for the Mammoth Mining Company Mill. From Mammoth Creek at the outlet of Twin Lakes, it circled around Panorama Dome, bringing water to power the Pelton Wheel that ran the twenty-stamp mill. From Mill City the combined waterways were named Mill Creek and continued downhill to the Mineral Park Sawmill and then into Mammoth Creek.

ACCOUNTS FROM OLD NEWSPAPERS.

Mammoth City, in 1879, boasted several news sheets, the *Mammoth City Herald, Mammoth City Times,* and *Lake Mining Review,* a weekly publication by Koole and Elliott. An original copy of the April 17, 1880 issue

 WATER WHEEL NEAR PINE CITY. The arrastra powered by the water wheel is out of sight. Mammoth Mountain shows faintly. The sidesaddle and ladies apparel indicate a very old photo, possibly the oldest Mammoth photo yet found. *Zelma Nelligan Photo.*

of the *Herald*—yellowed, wearing thin on the creases, but containing priceless bits of history—is on file in the Eastern California Museum at Independence. Its four pages were published twice weekly by Wm. B. Barnes and delivered in the three cities for 25¢ a week, $8.00 per year. Local agents were: W. H. Ellis, Bodie; L. E. Tubbs, Benton; J. H. Stoutenborough, Bishop Creek. The news column, headed "TAILINGS," included notes of the surrounding areas. Ads included business cards of surveyors, engineers, lawyers, a justice of the peace, and a surgeon-physician, Dr. P. J. Ragan. The paper also ran mine notices and ads for markets and hardware. Prominent were those for Gem Saloon, Mammoth Brewery, Mammoth Saloon, Nevada Saloon, Yosemite Saloon, The Lake View Mining Co., Yosemite Chop House, The California Hotel, The Lake House, and Fashion Stables. Out of town: Old Corner Saloon, Benton; Round Valley Flouring Mills, J. H. Jones.

A one-column ad extending the full length of the page listed in detail the goods carried by a general store, with this heading:

Geo. W. Rowan, dealer in GENERAL MERCHANDISE, South side of Mammoth Avenue (opposite the upper junction of the toll road) Respectfully calls the attention of his many friends of Mono county, also of Bishop Creek and Round Valley, to the fact that he has just received a large and well selected STOCK OF GENERAL MERCHANDISE.

From the same issue:

Alfred M'Millan, Photographer, Mammoth Avenue, adjoining Herald office. All kinds of portraits taken in the highest style of the art, and warranted to give perfect satisfaction. For sale—VIEWS of the MAGNIFICENT SCENERY in and around Mammoth City, constantly on hand.

From other issues of the *Herald*:

Pine City Feed and Livery Stable, corral and pasture attached, hay and grain for sale. PINE CITY—LAKE CITY. A share of trade solicited. *July 30, 1879.*

Fahey's Hotel, Main St., Mill City, J. M. Fahey, Prop. *October 22, 1879.*

In other issues of 1879 we find:

The fine library at the Temple of Folly will be opened as a circulating library tomorrow.

Mammoth City town lots are selling for $1500 for 25 foot frontage.

Another opium den is in the course of construction right in the center of town on main street.

Mammoth Brewery, Becker & Craytor, Proprietors, Most complete brewing establishment in this section. Pure cider a specialty. The best quality of wines, liquors and cigars. Beer by the measure, and furnished to the public in bottles or kegs.

Fred Brooks of Bishop gives some early history: "My father R. Fred Brooks was appointed COMMISSIONER OF DEEDS, (J.P.) at Mammoth City in 1879. He lived in a log cabin built among the little pines up Mammoth Ave., to the west. He had a small store and sold notions, various small supplies." While looking over photostatic copies of both the old papers at the Visitor Center, Mammoth Lakes, I found this ad in the *Herald* of October 22, 1879:

> R. Fred Brooks, bookseller, stationer and jeweler. Dealer in sheet music, school books, music instruments, combs, brushes, perfumery, guns, pistols and ammunition. Imported and domestic cigars supplied at wholesale to hotels, saloons and dealers. Wholesale and retail dealer for Continental Family Coal Oil, Being non-explosive, clear as water, and equal in brilliance to gas itself. R. Fred Brooks, No. 50 Main St., Mammoth City, Lake District, Cal; No. 38, North Carson St., Carson City, Nevada.

Noted in the second news sheet, *Mammoth City Times*, were items showing that pioneers, no matter where, managed to have happy times.

> Christmas Ball, to be given on the evening of Dec. 24, 1879 under the auspices of the Lake Dist. Pioneer Asso., at Giles Hall. Committee of arrangements; Rob't Delahide, John Pattie, T. J. Baker, Chas. Ball, Chas. Schuman. As this is an Institution Party there will be no charge for tickets. *December 18, 1879.*

> Mammothites believe in enjoying themselves. Two parties in a week speak well for their social proclivities. The installation ball of the Knights of Pythias, to occur tomorrow night in Giles Hall, will be a delightful party or we miss our guess, considerably. $3.00 is given as the price of tickets. *December 31, 1879.*

Another item records "a boat ride across Lake Mary to dance on a platform set up near the shore." One can almost hear those fiddles tuning up for a lively hoe-down, "gents you know, and a do se do," and the sounds of happy laughter echoing across the water.

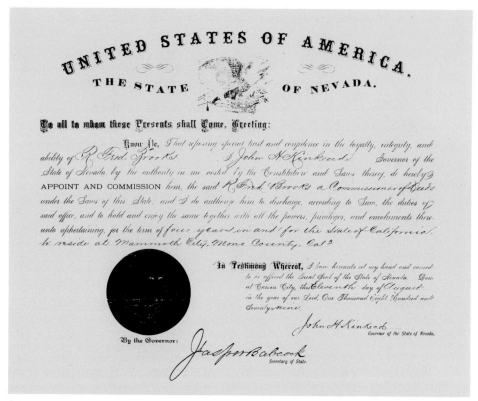

CERTIFICATE APPOINTING R. FRED BROOKS COMMISSIONER OF DEEDS AT MAMMOTH CITY,
August 11, 1879. Signed by the Governor of Nevada at Carson City. *Fred S. Brooks Collection.*

The papers indicate that the year 1879 saw the peak of activities, with mining at its maximum. The long and heavy snowfall during the winter of '79 and '80 brought hardships untold. Many decided it was *finis* for them. During 1880 the population of Mammoth City was estimated between 400 and 500. There was a general decline in mining, then came the heartbreak of fire, the enemy of most mining camps:

EXTRA, EXTRA.—DEVASTATION, the fire fiend at his work. Mammoth City nearly half in ruins. Families homeless, children destitute, loss near $45,000. CITIZENS IN COUNCIL! *Mammoth City Herald, November 15, 1880.*

By 1881 only a few prospectors lived on at Mammoth City.

RELICS OF LAKE MINING DISTRICT.

The foregoing gives insight into the life and activities during the few short years the "cities" flourished. It is all difficult to picture now, as these ghosty camps of over 100 years ago are marked by very few remains. Parts of two large log cabins are today the only remains of Mammoth City.

In the midst of a small clearing back of the Mill City Cabin Tract stands the only remaining in-place-relic of the Mammoth Mining Company. The massive iron flywheel of the 250-horsepower engine is still on its great shaft. The cylinder, two feet in diameter and with four-foot stroke, remains with its piston rod. According to Fred Brooks, the wheel was hauled in sections by twenty-mule team from Los Angeles in the 1870s and was bolted together on the spot. The mule skinner was Bert

THE 18-FOOT FLYWHEEL, at the ruins of the Mammoth Mining Co. mill. *Adele Reed Photo.*

Kingly, a relative of Albert Bodle. It was only due to the neighbors and the Forest Service that this historic flywheel remains at all. During World War II junk dealers were discovered salvaging all the old metal they could find and were stopped just in time.

TOM RIGG REMINISCES.

Tom Rigg, a valued friend and neighbor, was a scholarly English gentleman long addicted to prospecting and never happier than when roaming the great outdoors of our west. He lived, when not on his travels, with the Charles Summers family below Mammoth for many years.

I quote from letters sent us from Lone Pine, where he lived out his last years, letters written over the period from 1938 to 1946:

Dear Friends:

I often think of you folks as I sit in my yard staring at the hills and traveling once more, in imagination, the many trails I have wandered, happy memories. My first trip to Mammoth City was in 1892, Charlie Albright, Wildasinn and self went in a spring wagon. We had to pull out around snowbanks at the head of the old road going up from Casa Diablo. It was May 31st and Lake Mary was all frozen over and about 4 feet of snow around it and big drifts on the grade going up. Albright and self would go up to the cabin in Pine City every day, open it up and build fires in stove and fireplace to dry it out. The snow was higher than the log cabin, but by the Tom Price cabin on the road it was clear, the wind sweeps it off. Some years we could drive up to old Mammoth City at Christmas, but not with a car. Other years, fellows have left their wagons at the old sawmill on the creek till spring. Charlie Garretson left his there twice.

Mammoth sure sounds changed since I and Charlie Albright were the only summer residents up the hill. I worked nights in the hole and went sailing on Lake Mary afternoons, having patched up an old boat and cut up my bed canvas for a sail. Spent most of the time chasing "cats paws," would paddle up to one, only to have it die out, but would sometimes get a steady breeze. Some old-timers packed in some ½ inch lumber and tin objects from Grub Gulch and with these we built a punt about 8′ × 2½′ on upper Twin Lakes. The first fall I went out one morning when the ice was beginning to form and caught enough trout to fill a 3' keg, in about 3 hours. Took me longer to clean them than to catch them, none less than a foot long. Old Hill, that used to run the Valley View Hotel in Bishop sent up the keg and a sack of salt; he liked trout. Next day I took the keg down on a wheelbarrow to the old Sawmill and sent it down by a lumber team. There used to be some large fish in Redd's Lake. The best bait was live mice. Fasten a hook into one, float him out on a piece of bark, then jerk him off and you had a big one to handle.

A snowslide once carried two fellows down into Windy Flat from the Don Quiote or True Blue. They were working and got scared in a storm and started to come down the trail. You can see the two mine dumps up near the top in the recess above Monumental Rock.

I suppose the Monte Cristo is opening up, is anyone working the old Mammoth Mine or the Mahan Mine below the Lisbon? From the Mammoth to the Monte Cristo is a mine when it is opened up right, from Windy Flat. That is where the big working tunnel will start. The

THE MAMMOTH MINING COMPANY STAMP MILL. The huge wood supply was intended to fire a steam engine. The mill burned down in 1929. *Stephen Willard Photo.*

[[21]]

old Mammoth Mine was a 'get rich quick', they played stockholders instead of the mine, like many others. They spent a lot of money and when they did get a bunch of bonanza ore, they never got a nickel of it, it was all stolen. The Supt. and his gang got most, the 'trusties' got what they could. The head of the old company was known on the S. F. Stock exchange as 'Bilky Adams'. Everything was stock then, you paid for laundry, meals and so on, with stock. Charlie Albright used to get $20 a day and the tailings for rent of a 'spring-pole' mortar he had. After the company went broke, the Bank of Calif. took it over and let leasers work for nearly a year. Then the Bank closed everything out and the camp blew up.

Old Tom Agnew was recorder of the North Fork District, around Agnew Meadows, Shadow and Minaret Creeks and the head of the San Joaquin. He told me he saw about 20 sacks of the bonanza ore in the office one day, some open. Being a friend of the clerk he asked for a piece to assay. Tom said it went about $20,000 in gold and $40,000 in silver, pretty good pickings for Bilky and his pals!

Always remember to hole up in a bad storm and have plenty of wood in. Towards the end of Nov. keep one eye on the southeast.

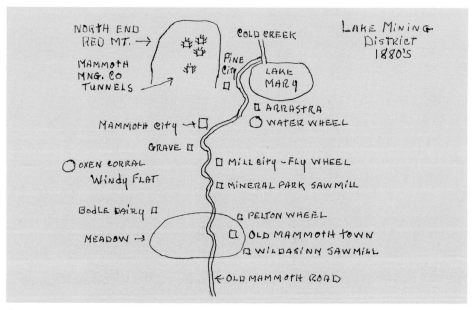

LAKE MINING DISTRICT IN THE 1880s. Sketch map by Adele Reed.

 THE 10-STAMP DOYLE MILL, built in 1898 at Mammoth City. *Stephen Willard Photo.*

When cirrus clouds begin to form, watch for the shut-in storm, and it usually means shutdown for the trails over the summit. It pays to treat the mountains with respect. A mail carrier went in on the Divide before you go down to the punch bowl, [on way to June Lake]. They found him in spring near an old stump and for several years after I came to Mammoth there was a big cross on it, hence the name, 'Deadman'. Well, best of luck to all and stop in when you can.

Cheerio, Tom Rigg

Very little is known of the in-between time, after the mines closed and before Mammoth Camp was built on the meadow. A few prospectors and miners lived on in the old camps and worked on claims here and there. The Doyle Mill, erected in 1898, promised new life for the mines. Dr. Guy Doyle of Bishop had the old Pelton wheel hauled up from Mill City to power his ten-stamp mill at Mammoth City. But again the mines did not pay, the mill closed and—little by little—time has erased all but a few traces of Lake Mining District and the mines on Mineral Hill.

Mammoth City, Cal. **Nov** 5ᵗʰ *1887*

Miss Watterson Bro

To **GEORGE STEVENS,** Dr.

DEALER IN

Stoves, Tin and Hardware, Sheet-Iron, Tinners' Supplies, Etc.

SOUTH SIDE OF MAIN STREET.

BODIE NEWS PRINT.

Aug 18 Scythe		1 12
1 2 lb ag Frugal Plate		2 50
3½ lbs Rivets		37
Strainer		1 25
Recd Payment		6 24
George Stevens		

✐ **BILL HEADING OF GEORGE STEVENS,** hardware dealer, Mammoth City. *Laura (Keough) Lutz Collection.*

✐ **PINE CITY CABIN.** No doubt one of the last remaining Pine City cabins noted by Tom Rigg. They were gone by the 1920s. *Frasher Collection, Pomona Public Library.*

☞ **THREE-STAMP MILL NEAR PINE CITY,** powered by water. Abandoned long ago, now vanished completely. *H. W. Mendenhall Photo.*

EARLY DAYS IN CALIF, NEAR MAMMOTH
H.W.M 997

THE TEMPLE OF FOLLY—IS THIS REALLY MAMMOTH CITY? This was long thought to be the only known photograph of Mammoth City in its boom days. There was no doubt that Mammoth had a Temple of Folly. Its ads occurred repeatedly in the *Mammoth City Times*: "Rock & Rye at the Temple of Folly. The new remedy for coughs, colds, etc. Everybody drinks it." [November 12, 1879]; and "All the citizens of Mammoth City, possessed of an enlightened curiosity, will learn with pleasure that the magnificent library in the 'Temple of Folly' is now open as a circulating library, commencing January 1st, 1880." [December 31, 1879].

Yet small misgivings remained. The lack of hills and pine trees in the background doesn't match with the site of Mammoth City. Nor do the bare trees behind the buildings look like aspen or willow, the only native deciduous trees there. Nor does any description of Mammoth City mention a boardwalk or substantial buildings such as these; quite the opposite. One visitor in 1880 described it as having ". . .the most temporary of temporary buildings—with a few exceptions. . ."

With the help of two lifetime residents of Bishop, in 1975, research has confirmed the misgivings and answered the question convincingly: the photograph is of Main Street in Bishop, probably in the 1890s. Elma Crosby has family memories as well as written evidence that A. J. Murphy and his wife (her Cousin Sarah) lived in Mammoth during 1879–80 and ran a saloon called the Temple of Folly. When they moved to Bishop, A. J. opened another Temple of Folly, commonly known as "Murphy's."

Comparing this photo with Bishop street scenes of around 1900 shows many similarities—a boardwalk, the design of the buildings, and *poplar* trees behind. Then Gus Cashbaugh pinned down this photograph, beyond all doubt, as the first block of North Main Street; he identified the town pump at the right-hand corner of Murphy's and the striped poles of Jake Koch's barber shop in the front of Murphy's—all of which he remembers clearly as a small boy in the 1890s.

Alas, this leaves us with no photograph at all of Mammoth City or any of the other Mammoth camps, though we keep hoping someone, someday, somewhere will yet discover the photographs Alfred M'Millan advertised in many issues of the *Mammoth City Herald.* —Ed.

PART III.

WAGON ROADS &
PACK TRAILS
TO MAMMOTH.

From earliest times, trails connected the native Paiute, Shoshone, and Washoe settlements that lay scattered along the base of the eastern Sierra. Trails also led west across Sierra passes, worn into the land by centuries of west- and east-slope Indian trading parties. The prospectors followed these old paths, as did the teamsters, cattlemen, merchants, and suppliers who came after them. They also broke many new trails to the mining camps. In time the steady march of horses hooves and iron-clad wagon wheels widened some of the trails into rough wagon roads. Many of our roads today follow these old routes.

STAGE LINES AND FREIGHT teams were truly the life lines of isolated mining camps such as the three little "cities" high up the eastern Sierra slope at the base of Mineral Hill, far distant from everywhere. Headquarters for much of the travel was the popular Monumental Hotel in Mammoth City. The newspapers constantly ran news items and ads about the comings and goings of teams and pack trains.

LAKE AND BODIE STAGE LINE, Carrying U. S. Mails and Wells, Fargo & Co.'s Express. Stages leave Mammoth City for King's Ranch and Bodie, Sundays, Wednesdays and Fridays. At 4 A.M. Time to Bodie, Where Close Connection is Made with the Carson Stage Line, Twelve Hours. Fare to Bodie, $15.

The CERRO GORDO Freighting Company will run teams into MAM-MOTH CITY, and can deliver freight from San Francisco by way of Mohave. Both news items above from the *Mammoth City Times, December 6, 1879.*

Charlie Ratcliffe arrived from San Francisco last night by the Fresno Flat route. To-day Mr. Ratcliffe is knocking about, but it is manifest that he has a tender regard for the seat of his trowsers. *Mammoth City Herald, July 30, 1879.*

H. H. Dickenson informs us that the road to Bishop Creek is now open for travel. He went to Gill's Station and back yesterday. Two ox teams and several large mule teams went over the road since the last storm. *Mammoth City Herald, November 22, 1879.*

A four horse wagon loaded with the finest of fresh fruit arrived in town last evening from the City of Los Angeles. In two or three days the last big freight team will arrive for this season. They will continue to bring freights for Mammoth as far as Bishop Creek and from that point will be forwarded with dispatch. *Mammoth City Herald, 1879.*

THE STAGE LINE FROM BODIE.

We like to think and wonder about the long run to Bodie—the four- and six-horse stages rattling and swaying down the rocky road, crossing the ford of Mammoth Creek, then heading northerly through forest country. At Deadman's Station they changed horses, then headed for King's Ranch where some stages stopped overnight. Next day the route led around the west side of Mono Lake to the Goat Ranch, for another change of horses, then a slow, uphill road to Bodie. According to a *Mammoth City Times:*

> Passengers on the Bodie Stage remark the large number of deer trails crossing the road near the Summit beyond Deadman's station, since the last snow. They all lead back into the mountains and we may therefore expect a season of fine weather. Mr. King, on the Bodie and Mammoth road has completed a fine large barn so is now able to house a larger number of horses in winter. *October, 1979.*

SHERWIN TOLL ROAD &
OTHER ROUTES FROM
BISHOP CREEK.

The southeasterly route used by teams and stages to Bishop Creek went from Mammoth City down to Sherwin and Laurel Creeks. It then followed the base of the mountains to McGee Meadows, Whisky Creek, Little Round Valley, Rock Creek and joined the toll road in Rock Creek Canyon. Fred Brooks recalled the toll road: "I used to go with my grandfather J. L. C. Sherwin on his trips to Mono Mills and Bodie when I was a boy. My aunt Nannie of Merced wrote me a letter. She told about how my grandfather built a road from Round Valley up and over the Sherwin Summit in the 1870s. He and other pioneers needed lumber for homes in Round Valley. He and associates, the Rowin brothers, James and Joseph, built sawmills in Rock Creek Canyon close to timber. In the late 1870s they continued the road up through the canyon and north. It was operated as the Sherwin Toll Road for several years."

In recent years a hand-drawn map by Fred Brooks was found in his memorabilia by his son Robert. It shows two other roads from Round

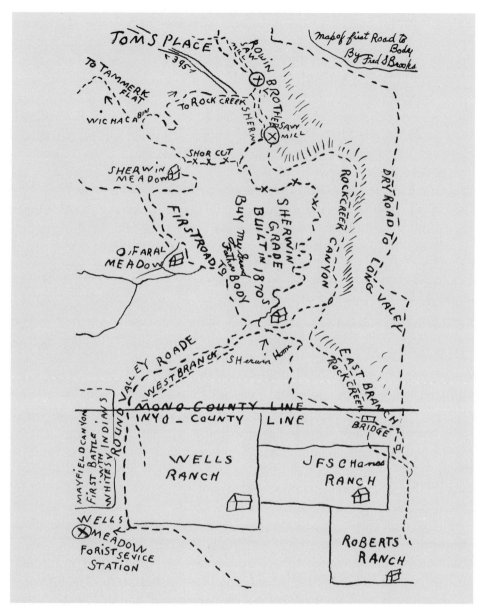

Map of first Road to Body
By Fred S Brooks

☝ **SKETCH MAP BY FRED S. BROOKS,** showing routes from Round Valley (north of Bishop) up Sherwin Grade to Tom's Place: the Sherwin Toll Road, the High Road to the west, and the Dry Road to the east. Whatever the route, Sherwin Grade was a long, hot, steep pull rising three thousand feet above the valley. To make the map easier to read, color Rock Creek and both its branches blue and then trace each wagon route with a different color. Fred's map is remarkably accurate. The routes shown match astonishingly well with the wagon roads on the 1912 and 1914 topographic maps of this area. Today's four-lane Highway 395 follows the general route of the Dry Road. *Fred S. Brooks Collection.*

Valley north. The High Road was built from Round Valley and Sherwin Meadows for winter use. The route was by the Wicha Cabin and Spring, once a Ranger Station used by the Forest Service, thence to Rock Creek Station connecting with the toll road.

The exact location of the Dry Road is elusive. It was used for travel to Long Valley, Mammoth City, and Bodie when deep snow in Rock Creek Canyon or on the High Road halted travel. It turned off right from old Highway 395 near the Roberts Ranch and rock silo and led north, keeping east of Rock Creek Canyon and west of the Owens River Gorge. It joined the main road at Little Round Valley. Other times when snow closed all three roads, the Benton Hot Springs, McLaughlin Canyon, Little Antelope route to Casa Diablo and Mammoth City might be snow-free.

Philip P. Keough, grandfather of Laura (Keough) Lutz, was superintendent of the United Stage Company, a branch of the Wells Fargo Express. His "Fast Freight" made regular trips to Mammoth City, Bodie, and Aurora by another route. Headquarters, stock, barn, corrals, and the main depot were located at Fish Slough, about eight miles north of Bishop Creek. After picking up passengers in town and loading at the depot, they set out for Old Benton by way of Yellowjacket Spring. Adobe Meadows, the next stop-over, was a small settlement 'mid haying and cattle country. William Symons, Jr. recalls that it was a very important source of hay and beef for the mining camps. From Adobe Meadows, roads led in many directions. The main road led north directly to Aurora. A branch from this turned west, ending at Bodie. Another branch road took off westerly through the hills and canyons, crossed the Owens River near the Arcularius Ranch, followed Long Valley and then turned up the road by Laurel Creek to reach the mining camps.

Arrival of the stage was always a big event. No road was too rough or weather too bad, the stage must go through! However, heavy snows made it impossible for the stage to get through to Mammoth City from early January to March 17, 1881. Accordingly, the United Stage Company had $213 deducted from their pay as mail contractor, as noted in the accompanying Post Office document. This bad winter, after the very deep snows of the winter before, coupled with the discouraging turn of events in 1880—the mill closing and the fire—spelled the end of the three little cities of Lake Mining District.

(FORM 2211.)

Post Office Department,

OFFICE OF THE SECOND ASSISTANT POSTMASTER GENERAL,

Division of Inspection,

June 4, 1881.

SIR:

A deduction of $ *213, 30* has been ordered from your pay as Contractor on Route No. *46,323*, in the State of *California*, for the quarter ended *March 31*, 1881, because of failure *at Mammoth, to arrive Jany 5, 7, 12, 17, 21, 28, 31, to depart Jan 1, 6, 8, 13, 18, 22, 29, to arrive Feb. 4, 11, 16, 21, 25, to depart Feb. 5, 12, 17, 22, 26, to arrive Mch 2, 9, 16, to depart Mch. 3, 10, 17, 1881,*

This deduction has been ordered in accordance with the stipulation in your contract by which it is agreed that you shall forfeit: "(1.) The pay of a trip when it is not run, and, in addition, if no sufficient excuse for the failure is furnished, an amount not more than three times the pay of the trip." No pay, therefore, can be allowed for a trip not performed. Whatever obstacle may have prevented its performance, the *price of the trip must be deducted*; and if a *satisfactory* excuse is not received, *more than the price* (not exceeding three times) may be deducted. Contractors will see the importance, therefore, in cases of failure, of forwarding *immediately*, to the Division of Inspection, any excuse they may have to offer. Such excuse must state, *specifically*, the cause of the failure, and whether any, and, if any, what effort was made to perform the trip; and if *part* of it was performed, *what part* must be stated, and the distance given. All the facts stated must be verified by the *oath* of the party having a personal knowledge of them, or by the certificate of a Postmaster who may be cognizant of the facts. Attention to these requirements will frequently prevent annoyance to you as Contractor, and also to the Department, by enabling this Office to properly adjust the fines and deductions.

Respectfully,

R. A. Elmer

Second Assistant Postmaster General.

To *N. H. Pease Esq,*
Contractor,
Atchison
Atchison Co,
Kans.

✍ POST OFFICE DOCUMENT, June 4, 1881. Deduction from mail contractor's pay for failure to deliver mail to Mammoth City during the winter of 1881. *Laura (Keough) Lutz Collection.*

THE FRESNO FLATS TRAIL.

A 100-mile long pack trail ran from the town of Fresno across the Sierra to Mammoth City. According to history, it was once a toll-way named the Old French Trail. During the mining boom in Lake District it also became known as the Fresno Flats Trail, for one of the overnight stops along the route was at Fresno Flats, in the foothills east of Fresno. Early prospectors followed the trail from the west side to Jackass, Iron Mountain, and the Minarets, looking for minerals. As late as the 1930s the trail was used by prospectors, Indians, sheepmen, and Forest Service crews.

The mud baths and hot springs on the trail, at the South Fork of the San Joaquin River, were popular meeting places for Indians from the west and Paiutes from the east. They believed that the springs were cures for certain troubles. They also met to trade—obsidian for arrowheads and cutting points, salt, and pine nuts from the east traded for acorns, baskets, and shell beads from the west.

During the mining boom in Lake District, the Fresno Flats Pack and Saddle Train kept the trail busy, transporting mining men back and forth from San Francisco and hauling produce and supplies from Fresno. Headquarters for the pack train was the Monumental Hotel on Central Mammoth Avenue. According to the newspapers:

> The Monumental Hotel, Central Mammoth Avenue, The Leading Hotel of Mammoth City. This hotel is the headquarters of San Francisco and Bodie travel, and is first class in every respect. The Fresno Flats saddle train arrives and departs from our door. *Mammoth City Herald, July 30, 1879.*

> LAKE DISTRICT AND FRESNO FLATS SADDLE TRAIN. Leaves Mammoth City Tuesdays and Fridays at 5 A.M. Leaves Fresno Flats same days on arrival of the Medara stages. Twenty pounds of baggage free. Freight from Fresno Flats to Mammoth 8¢. Fare to Fresno Flats, $15.00 Fare to Medara, $20.00 Fare to San Francisco, $29.00 *Mammoth City Herald, July 30, 1879.*

> A mixed train of fifteen mules, horses and jacks came in from the western slope Sunday last, loaded with produce, returning the same day. *Mammoth City Times, 1880.*

The year 1876–77 was a drought year in western California. Along this trail (and many others) flocks of sheep and herds of horses were trailed into Sierra meadows. When it came time to gather and trail out, corrals were built at a place that became known as 77 Corral. A family named

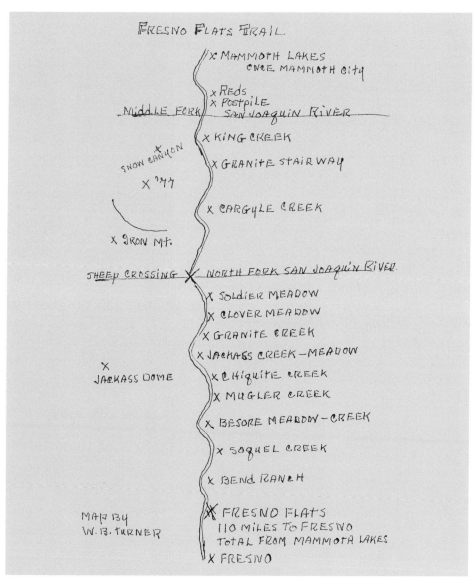

FRESNO FLATS TRAIL

x MAMMOTH LAKES
ONCE MAMMOTH CITY

x Reds
x Postpile
SAN JOAQUIN RIVER

MIDDLE FORK

x KING CREEK

SNOW CANYON

x GRANITE STAIRWAY

X ?77

x CARGYLE CREEK

x IRON Mt.

SHEEP CROSSING X NORTH FORK SAN JOAQUIN RIVER.

x SOLDIER MEADOW
x CLOVER MEADOW
x GRANITE CREEK
x JACKASS CREEK — MEADOW
x CHIQUITE CREEK
x MUGLER CREEK

X
JACKASS DOME

x BESORE MEADOW — CREEK

x SOQUEL CREEK

x BEND RANCH

MAP BY
W. B. TURNER

X FRESNO FLATS
110 MILES TO FRESNO
TOTAL FROM MAMMOTH LAKES

X FRESNO

FRESNO FLATS TRAIL MAP. Sketched by Bill Turner and re-drawn by Adele Reed.

Turner, who lived near Fresno, sheeped the meadows along the trail for many years. Their son Bill rode the trail in 1910 and 1917 and then through the 1920s, making trips out to the Summers store at Old Mammoth when he needed supplies.

In the 1920s and '30s the Forest Service used the trail for access from both east and west. A District Ranger during the summer season divided his time between the Clover Meadow and Reds Meadow stations (twenty miles apart), for at that time the Sierra National Forest extended to the Mammoth Crest Divide. At a difficult crossing of the North Fork of the San Joaquin River, the Forest Service built a swinging bridge. Named Sheep Crossing, at first the bridge was used without rails and was quite hazardous. Our information on this trail came from three men: Bill Turner of Fresno, John McGee, and Lee Verret. The last two, who worked during the summer at Reds Meadow for the Forest Service, were very interested in the early use of the historic Fresno Flats Trail.

In 1924 Bill Reed accompanied Roy Boothe, then assistant Forest Supervisor on the Sierra Forest, on a two-week inspection trip. They rode some of the old trail checking stock and feed, meeting cattlemen and covering a great area. They also used several of the old stop-over camps: Jackass Meadows, 77 Corral, and at Fresno Flats they found a cabin and a corral with a small stream of water. It had seen of use by humans and livestock. The trail, worn deep by many iron-clad hooves, was easily followed from Mammoth City, passing close to Horseshoe and McLeod Lakes, dropping over the summit to Reds Meadow, crossing the Middle Fork of the San Joaquin, climbing up to Summit Meadow, and continuing on west—a ride through superb scenery and forest.

☞ THE FIRST ROAD OVER SHERWIN SUMMIT, built in the 1870s by Jim Sherwin and associates to their sawmills in Rock Creek Canyon. The mining boom at Mammoth spurred them to extend their road north through the canyon and operate it as the Sherwin Toll Road. Over this road ox teams and mule teams pulled heavy freight wagons between Bishop Creek and Mammoth. These ruts, worn deeply into the rock by thousands of iron-rimmed wagon wheels, endure to this day. *Don Bell Collection.*

 THE SWINGING BRIDGE AT SHEEP CROSSING, west of Mammoth, North Fork of the San Joaquin River. Built by the Forest Service in the 1920s. *Rose Boothe Collection.*

 SUMMER GRAZING IN THE HIGH SIERRA. Shepherds drove their flocks up to the high mountain meadows in summer. A common sight in earlier days.

"THE OLD STYLE"
BOULDER LODGE, JUNE LAKE

☝ ROCK CREEK STATION, a stop on the Bishop Creek-Bodie-Carson City stage line in the late 1870s. Pictured is a typical stage used on the short lines; it did not have the rock-away comfort of the long-line coaches. According to Swan Wilson, a descendant of owners of Swall Meadow, "The route south and over the Toll Road was a rough one, hard on stage travelers. Sometimes they pulled in at Sherwin Meadow to rest and some would camp overnight." *U. S. Forest Service Photos.*

☝ OLD STAGE, JUNE LAKE. A venerable stage of the same type stood for long years at June Lake. Slim Tatum, owner in the 1930s of the Frontier Pack Outfit, Silver Lake, was asked to haul the stage to Boulder Lodge. He recalls, "I got together a broke team of six animals and drove around to Silver Lake and back to the lodge with passengers! The old stage stood there, then disappeared, no one knew when or where it went."

PART IV.

MAMMOTH
IN THE MEADOW
1900–1937.

When the bonanza didn't materialize, the Mammoth Mining Company shut down its mill early in 1880, company stock became worthless, and the property sold at a sheriff's sale. Just a few years later, in 1888, H. A. Whiting reported that ". . . half a dozen prospectors are all that now remain of a population estimated at fifteen hundred souls in 1879." As far as we know, during the next twenty years the only other people in Mammoth were the cowhands who drove cattle from Owens Valley up into the mountain meadows for summer and fall grazing. It wasn't until the 1900s that a different breed of pioneer discovered Mammoth.

T WAS A DIFFERENT breed of pioneer who settled and built the little village in the meadow. Pioneers, none-the-less, who came in those "funny" old cars. Instead of the clip, clop of shod hooves and the rumble and rattle of wagons up the creek road, now the woods echoed to the strange sounds of the latest inventions. Fords, Chevies, E.M.F.'s (Every Morning Fix-it), and others—vintage 1914 on up. They made it through the desert, up the rough roads, steep grades, by dint of all hands pushing at times when the motor got too hot, or the radiator boiled, or the car just coughed and died! These pioneers had several things in common: love of their beautiful "chosen land;" youth in abundance; and little worldly goods or coin-of-the-realm. They were eager, worked hard, played hard, and "made do" the best they could. For many years it was rather a remote area, so they made their own fun. Any event called for a celebration—dancing, pot-luck dinners, a party—all hilarious good fun.

The country was primitive, wild and attractive. The gem-like lakes and snow-capped mountains above were an elegant backdrop for the village that grew in the midst of a meadow ringed by fragrant forests. In spring and summer, tall grasses waved and bright spots of flowers added vivid color. Mammoth Creek, noisy and rushing in spring and meandering lazily in summer, cut a curving path through the middle of grassland. It was bordered thickly by willows and aspen and full of wary trout. The deep, dark holes were tricky to fish. Deer, mountain quail, grouse in the wooded areas, sagehen on the flats, and ducks and geese on the waterways below—it was a sportsman's paradise.

THE WILDASINN HOTEL,
MAMMOTH'S FIRST RESORT: EARLY 1900S.

Among the first to acquire land in this paradise was Charles F. Wildasinn, who built the first resort in Mammoth, date unknown. "He was a wise man!" said Fred Brooks, shaking his head. "Land was open for home-steading in the 1800s and C. F. Wildasinn was one who took advantage and filed on 160 acres of meadowland. He built a small hotel, a store, a sawmill by the creek, and a fine log cabin for his own use. He also acquired many small parcels of timber land under the Timber Culture Act."

In the earliest days this general area was known as Mineral Park and extended from the meadow to the foot of the grade below Mill City. As the name keeps popping up, a few notes are of interest. An early map in the Ben Noxon collection, author unknown, has the name Mineral Park Hotel and Store. Gus Cashbaugh of Bishop recalled, "The summer of 1893 I went with my father, hauling produce by wagon and team from his ranch up to the people living in tents at Mineral Park below Mill City."

Hearing of a former guest of the hotel, with picture in hand we visited Dorothy (Doyle) Cook one summer at Lake George. Dorothy has vivid memories of staying at the hotel as a child. She took one look at the picture and said, "Oh my, it's so true to life it makes me sad. I could cry!" Dorothy's parents were the well known Dr. Guy and Dr. Helen Mac-Knight Doyle of Bishop who spent vacations with their family at the Wildasinn Hotel in 1906, '07 and '08. "What a wonderful place Mammoth was for youngsters as we were. The two-story hotel had a steep, narrow stairway to the four guest rooms. The lobby was artistically decorated with a frieze of red-brown manzanita branches all around the burlap covered walls. Gorgeous! It was done by a relative who came to visit Uncle Charlie and Aunt Sarah. There was a little store nearby where we could find most anything. One of the cabins in the trees back of the hotel was owned by a Mr. Hampton. There were several others."

The hotel had a register covering the years 1908–1911 that is now in the Mono County Museum. (Fred Brooks always believed the resort dated back to the mining era.) The Wildasinn log cabin has an addition now, but still stands 'mid tall aspens close to the Pelton wheel. The huge rock fireplace in the original cabin, with smoke-blackened mantle and wall, relates to the early years.

Our friend Tom Rigg, already mentioned, knew Mammoth during these years also. In one of his letters, he describes the summer he grazed cattle in Deer Creek's meadows on the west slope of Mammoth Crest, probably driving them over Mammoth Pass.

In the summer of 1914 I was working for Tom Williams at Windy Flat where he had cattle. I took the cows over to Deer Creek, he had a permit. I packed in some wire and put up a paddock to keep a couple of horses, it was where the upper trail crosses the creek, guess it is all gone now. Jim Nevins stayed at Windy Flat to irrigate whilst I was away. I would ride over to Mammoth once a week to get supplies and mail. When War One started I left and Tommy fetched up Gerald McLeod to take my place. I went to Bishop with Charlie Summers and from there to Frisco. Then by boat to Victoria and signed on with the Gordons (Canada), 'for overseas' Sept. 10th.

 CHARLES F. WILDASINN, pioneer of Old Mammoth. His log cabin, pictured above, still stands in the aspen trees at the edge of the meadow. *Ben Noxon Collection.*

✍ OLD MAMMOTH IN THE EARLY 1900S. THE WILDASINN HOTEL AND STORE. With this one extraordinary photograph it takes little imagination to picture the time and the place that was Old Mammoth. The buildings on the far right are Mammoth's first resort, the Wildasinn Hotel and Store. Charlie Wildasinn also built a sawmill on Mammoth Creek and a log cabin for himself that is half hidden in the aspen trees. Roofs of a few cabins belonging to other people show through the trees. In 1918 Charles Summers chose the area just left of the hotel to build his own larger hotel and rooming house, Mammoth Camp.

In the foreground is a small portion of the huge meadow that long provided summer pasture for cattle and horses. The view from the meadow is southwest toward Mammoth Crest, the flat-topped ridge in the center distance. Mammoth Crest's altitude is 10,600 feet; the meadow's, 7850 feet.

The long ridge on the skyline to the left, Mineral Hill (Red Mountain) can take credit for the gold-mining boom that first attracted white men here and for giving the land its name, *Mammoth*, from the Mammoth Mining Company. On the far side of Mineral Hill, prospectors discovered gold ore in 1877. On the rubbly slope of Mineral Hill's north face, the Mammoth Mining Company dug four tunnels (still quite recognizable today, one above the other) and built a tramway from the tunnels to its mill over half a mile away. At the base of the slope grew Mammoth City, the largest of the mining camps.

Monumental Rock (now Mammoth Rock), the pale gray limestone crag on the east slope of Mineral Hill, gave its name to one of Mammoth City's popular spots, the Monumental Hotel.

Between Mineral Hill and Mammoth Crest lies a broad flat-bottomed basin, the Lakes Basin, whose scenic beauty has elicited lyrical comments since the earliest mining days. Owens Valley people discovered its magnificent scenery long before Big City people; Old Mammoth's earliest summer cabins were built by residents of Bishop and other Valley towns.

Broad-shouldered Mammoth Mountain looms up on the right. On its lower east slopes, pictured above, small ski tows operated sporadically during the 1940s.

The historic wagon road in the photograph was first traveled by the freight wagons and teams that supplied the old mining camps. Later, fishermen and tourists traveled the same road to reach the Lakes Basin. Today's Old Mammoth Road follows essentially the same route.

Unfortunately for us, Andrew Forbes, the photographer, did not date his photos—or if he did, his records long ago disappeared. However, from what we know of him, he most likely took this picture sometime between 1902 and 1916. The three automobiles left of the hotel indicate the later years, probably around 1910. *A. A. Forbes Photo.*

FRED BROOKS REMINISCES.

Fred, long a resident of Bishop, was the historian of Old Mammoth days, for he knew it in its infancy. He was born in Round Valley in 1885 and remembers traveling with his grandfather to the mountain areas when but a boy. His mother, May Sherwin Brooks, told him much history of the old days. Her father, J. L. C. Sherwin, was prominent in the early days of Inyo-Mono. Many feet have trod the little path into Fred's home, people in search of authentic data, which he gives eagerly.

Prior to 1907 he was riding as a cowboy for Summers and Butler with headquarters at Laurel Creek. "If it was near noon and we were working thereabouts, we'd head for the old Wildasinn Hotel to eat. There was a family running it and the women did the cooking, only charged two-bits for a meal!" In 1907 he worked for the Forest Service and would ride from Well's Meadow in Round Valley to the mountains. In 1917 he and his wife, Stella, became residents of Old Mammoth. With his background of about eight years of work in the W. L. Smith store in Bishop, Charlie Summers picked him to come up and run the Wildasinn store as a beginning. Charlie had purchased all of the Wildasinn holdings but the personal log cabin. Fred and Stella lived in the little lean-to by the old store that season. He was storekeeper at Mammoth from 1917 to 1934.

This is how Fred remembers Mammoth Camp in '17 and '18. "We had to wait until May to get in as the snow was too deep. The mail was brought up from Bishop by anyone they could find headed this way. It was a big sack and we sorted and put it in little cubbyholes for people to pick up. There was no cancellation at that time, as it was not officially a post office. Supplies were hauled by truck and that included gasoline for the few cars coming in. The gas was in 50-gallon drums and a 5-gallon can with a spout was used to fill cars. The can had the gallons marked, and the car owners would take a measuring stick from under the front seat and measure the tank (under the seat usually) so I could tell how many gallons to draw from the drum.

"In 1918, Charlie Summers built a new hotel, rooming house, and cabins. Stella and I moved into a cabin. The new store was built a little later and it was farther down the meadow just across Mammoth Creek from the old sawmill site. The big barn and corrals were across the road from the store, to the west. A gasoline storage tank was installed at the new store and a one-gallon hand pump stood on the porch. Cars had to drive close or back close, depending on where their tank was, at the rear or under the front seat. It took a lot of time, having to pump up each gallon."

Fred remembered sledding the old Pelton wheel from Mammoth City down to its present site on a ditch from Mammoth Creek to generate power for the Wildasinn Hotel. It took two sets of primitive sleds, made of logs lashed together, and six mules to haul it down grade. (This is the same water wheel that first supplied power to the Mammoth Mining Company Mill and twenty years later powered the Doyle Mill.) Finally Charlie Summers hooked it up to supply electricity to his new resort, Mammoth Camp.

THE 6-FOOT PELTON WHEEL that generated electricity for Wildasinn's Hotel. *A. Reed Photo.*

THE SUMMERS FAMILY:
MAMMOTH CAMP, 1918—1927.

Fred described the handsome Summers Hotel: "It was built of logs cut near Twin Lakes. They were hauled down to the Sawmill and slabbed on two sides to make them flat. They were held together by large steel spikes. The building was about 40 × 80 feet and the big lobby was across the front with a double fireplace square in the center. A big dining room was next and the kitchen, built of lumber, was back of that. There were long seats about the fireplace and chairs, and fine, framed pictures hung on the walls. A wide, roofed porch, supported by big peeled logs, extended all across the front, and there were several rocking chairs waiting for visitors. Charlie used to sit there in nice weather and visit. The hotel was the gathering place for cabin people too."

Olive Barker was visiting with Charlie on the porch one bright spring day when a big car drove up. "It was the kind with big leather seats and lots of shiny metal trim," Olive remembered. A chauffeur came to Charlie and asked about rooms. He replied yes, he had rooms (the 30 rooms were in a separate two-story building beside the hotel). When asked to send someone out for the luggage, Charlie's explosive answer was typical. "Hell, no! Everyone waits on themselves in this country!" Olive explained, "He never really wanted to run a hotel, he was a cattleman."

This was true, he was raised in the life of the range. He and brothers John, Jim, and Tom originally came from a big valley in Sierra County, leaving one brother, Will, on the home place. Charlie and John settled in Long Valley, on land that extended from Laurel Creek to Casa Diablo Hot Springs. The two bought the Rawson holdings, including a roomy log cabin and corrals. Charlie and Libby later lived in a cabin among the trees up Laurel Creek. After the boys married, two of them built nearby. Lloyd and Sybil (McGee) lived west of Laurel, where their cabin still stands. Len and wife Evalina (Evans) built just across the creek on the Rawson side. Brother John and wife Eva (Wells) built their own home over near Hot Creek. It is now known as the Chance cattle headquarters.

Charlie's sons and families were included in and helped with the hotel and pack business he started in 1918, Mammoth Camp. Charlie, the youngest son, and his wife Altha (Branson) of Big Pine later ran the Agnew Meadow Pack Camp. In the early 20s many changes began to appear—new cabin people up the creek, more campers and fishermen, and gradually a new business here and there. At the store an inside corner was partitioned off, a window with shelf, and a little cast-iron wood heater for comfort—this was the Mammoth Lakes Post Office. No longer was the mail brought in hit or miss fashion as in the first days. The Summers truck made daily trips to Bishop for mail and supplies until other arrangements were made. In 1923 passengers came to Mammoth Camp by the Bishop-Mono Lake Auto Stage Line. Lloyd Summers was the first postmaster and his wife Sybil then took the office at Old Mammoth until 1937, when it was moved to the new highway. In the winter of 1927 a disastrous fire wiped out most of Mammoth Camp. However, the Summers name remains an important part of Old Mammoth tradition.

☛ **Elizabeth (Gunter) McGee And, Below, Her Husband, Cattleman Alney McGee,** pioneers of Inyo and Mono counties. Their daughter Sybil married Lloyd Summers and raised their sons (Lee, Verne, and Dick) at Mammoth. *Rhys May Collection.*

☞ **Mammoth Camp, 1918 To 1927.** Two-story rooming house, left; Summers Hotel, built of logs cut near Twin Lakes, right. *H. W. Mendenhall Photo.*

☛ **(Grandma) Elizabeth Summers,** wife of Charles, in her rocking chair on the hotel porch. *Florence (Huckaby) Smith Collection.*

Grandmother McGee. Allie's wife. Trix May's Mother.

Allie McGee. Inyo County Pioneer.

Mammoth Camp

 THE SUMMERS FAMILY, at their Laurel Creek cabin and log corrals. Charles, Elizabeth, and their sons Len, Lloyd, and Charlie Jr. Charles and John Summers bought C. B. Rawson's holdings—land extending from Laurel Creek to Casa Diablo Hot Springs. *Photos from Verne Summers Collection.*

✑ **Fourth Of July At Mammoth Camp.** The Fourth was usually celebrated with a hotly contested ball game or an exciting rodeo. From extreme left to right: the barn and corrals, rooming house, Summers Hotel with roofed porch, old Wildasinn Hotel, Summers Store. On the porch of the store, note the one-gallon hand pump for gasoline. "It took a lot of time, having to pump up each gallon!" said Fred Brooks. *Laura (Keough) Lutz Collection.*

☞ **Charlie Summers At Laurel Creek,** pioneer cattleman turned hotel-keeper, builder of Mammoth Camp. The Summers family gave warmth and personality to Old Mammoth days. Although fire destroyed Mammoth Camp in 1927, the Summers name remains an important part of Old Mammoth tradition. *Ernest Kinney Collection.*

THE MCGEE FAMILY.

Other names closely connected with Old Mammoth were those of Frank Butler and Alney L. McGee. Frank Butler, stepson of Jim Butler who discovered Tonopah, Nevada in 1900, was Charlie Summers' partner in the cattle business in Long Valley in early times. Alney McGee used to ride with Summers and Butler. A brief "look" into Alney's life from the McGee family history by Eva (McGee) Yaney: "Alney McGee, born in Texas in 1844, traveled west in a covered wagon with his family, trailing a herd of longhorns, finally settling in Inyo-Mono. Their cattle ranged the McGee Creek and Adobe Meadow areas. Hence, the name McGee was given to the mountain and creek in Long Valley, a creek at Adobe and "Little McGee" near Bishop. Alney and brother Bart were famous Indian fighters in Owens Valley, and Bart operated a stage station near McGee Creek in Long Valley when Mammoth City was booming.

"In September 1853, Elizabeth (Gunter) McGee was born in a covered wagon at a camp high up in the Sierra Nevada mountains. The spot was known as Emigrant Gap on the Placerville road. A baby girl was born! And the wagons rolled on, to a new home in Sacramento, California. Later Elizabeth came to Bishop and in 1870 she became the wife of Alney. They raised four children: Eva, Mrs. W. P. Yaney; Beatrice, Mrs. Clyde May; Sybil, Mrs. Lloyd Summers; and Percy McGee. Sybil's children, Lee, Verne and Dick, were raised at Mammoth. Beatrice May's daughter, Beatrice ('Sis'), married Cecil Thorington, sheriff of Mono County for many years. The eldest May son, Rhys, was a long time resident of Old Mammoth."

OLD GRAVES.

Reports of two graves near the edge of Windy Flat have, for long years, kept cropping up. Who were these persons? Were they the two unlucky miners caught in a snow slide from far up back of Monumental Rock (as noted in Tom Rigg's letter)? Were they the only remainder of a pioneer burial ground? Who can tell us?

Deciding to see for ourselves, we hiked some of the area adjacent to the Flat. Over a little hill, nestled on a manzanita covered slope we found the two cement headstones, side by side. After reading the two inscriptions, the mystery continued. Our first thought had been, the two unlucky miners! However the dates were not right. It was Fred Brooks who supplied the answer: "Sure, I remember him. Gibbs was one of the first campers in Shady Rest. He decided Mammoth was to be his home, even tried to buy out Charlie Summers. He did buy an acre or so from Charlie near Windy Flat. He had his father's body brought there from southern California for reburial in their private graveyard." Smaller graves, now unmarked, were family pets. The inscriptions as follows:

Clarence M. Gibbs. Oct. 2, 1880–Aug. 13, 1922
FATHER Joseph H. Gibbs, 1843–1883

In a heavily wooded spot between Mill City and Windy Flat was the graveyard of the three mining camps. It was a peaceful, beautiful, woodsy area. Little picket fencings, weathered and faded headboards—nameless—midst brush and rocks, was the scene we found at the end of a long hike many years ago.

In the early '50s Bishop residents, Louis and Joe Serventi, accompanied by Fred Brooks, gave time and effort to erect a cement monument there. It was placed in the midst of the only group of four or five graves that could be located by that time. Facing to the east, its inscription read, "WE WILL NEVER FORGET YOU." Firmly cementing it to a heavy base, the donors hoped it would remain a permanent tribute to our pioneers. However, vandals have desecrated it as well as the old Townsend grave above Mill City Camp. Louis Serventi said, "We have tried for many years to repair the damage to the Townsend grave each year, but it is becoming a useless struggle and we are discouraged."

SAWMILLS NEAR MAMMOTH.

One of the most important industries in early times, especially in remote mining areas, was a nearby sawmill. It could supply anything needed to build a home or business. Located along the old road into the mining camps, three mills supplied lumber during the mining boom. The Rawson Mill, named for a cattleman of early Inyo-Mono, C. B. Rawson, whose name was also given to the lower meadows, was on Laurel Creek. The Sherwin Shake and Shingle Mill, owned by J. L. C. Sherwin, was located above the road, just before it crossed Sherwin Creek. The Mammoth Steam Sawmill Company was in Mineral Park, at the foot of the grade and about one-half mile below Mill City. The mill was located beyond the present Pine Cliff Resort, very near Mill Creek. The original old horse-and-wagon road turned left just above the entrance to Pine Cliff Resort and angled up a steep grade to Mill City, keeping left of Mill Creek. (The present road was graded through the mill site.) Logging was carried on throughout the park, from Mammoth Creek on up through the canyon of Mill Creek and from Mill City easterly to the bluffs overlooking Windy Flat. The mill advertised a variety of lumber:

MAMMOTH STEAM SAW MILLS, MINERAL PARK
At the foot of the new Mammoth City Grade

These Mills are prepared to furnish LUMBER in quantities from 500 to 100,000 feet at short notice. There is now on hand a large quantity of seasoned FLOORINGS, BATTINGS, SHINGLES and other DEPENDABLE BUILDING MATERIAL adapted to the wants of the community. Orders filled promptly and lumber delivered, when desired, to any part of Mammoth, Mill, or Pine City.

MAMMOTH STEAM SAWMILL COMPANY. *Mammoth City Herald, April 17, 1880.*

Fred Brooks' mother told her sons how the lumber was freighted: "Remi Nadeau, the famed early day freighter lived in a log cabin in Old Mammoth about where the red and white Arcularius house now stands, near the Bodle cabin. Nadeau kept 16 to 20 oxen in a big log corral farther up Windy Flat and across in the trees [the corral was located where Fred and his brother used to fish in the little lake, just beyond]. The teams of oxen were used to haul freight and lumber up to the mining camps."

Lower down in the meadow on the north side of Mammoth Creek was the Wildasinn Mill. The exact date of its origin remains unknown, but there is no evidence that it operated during the mining boom. The road to this mill crossed the creek at the old ford just above the mill. The Wildasinn Mill was sold in 1908 to the Home Lumber Company and moved into the timber beyond what is now Shady Rest Campground. A ditch from Mammoth Creek, Sawmill Ditch, brought water through the woods and close to the campground.

Florence (Huckaby) Smith of Bishop told us of her years at Mammoth around this time. Her family, the George Huckabys, moved to the

Owens Valley from the east in 1874 and settled in Laws, near Bishop. "In about 1910, my Dad and brothers, Frank, Charles, and Claude had a timber lease from Wildasinn. They cut and hauled logs by team for the Home Lumber Company. Horses were also used at that time to load the logs on the big wagons. I will never forget the summers at Mammoth. Mother and my sisters and I would join Father and the boys after school was out. It was the best time of the year for us, in fact, the most enjoyable of our lives together. We roamed the woods as free as wild colts and there were flowers and birds and meadowland to explore. How we did hate to leave in the early fall—school, studies and shoes on our feet!" This life continued until Wildasinn sold the land to Charles Summers in 1917.

The Home Lumber Company sold to Fred M. Hess and Arthur W. Hess of Bishop in 1920, and thereafter the mill was known as Hess Lumber Company. The brothers Hess acquired, along with the mill and equipment, two sets of "Big Wheels,"—go-devils, very picturesque and also capable of hauling heavy logs from the especially rough areas. "These were manufactured in Manistee, Michigan in 1875," as noted in *Spinning Wheel,* December 1961, "and sold for $150 to $300 a pair. Six California firms were using them by 1893, however, they have gradually disappeared, and now if a pair is found it is museum material."

"The Big Wheels were in the area when we took over," Art Hess relates, "and I believe they were shipped in from Martell, a prominent lumbering area on the west side. We used them for a year or so and one pair was sold in Los Angeles. Possibly the other ones ended as sign-holders in front of the Crestview Lodge." These sign-holders were a historical landmark of Mono County for many years. The wheels, ten feet in diameter, were made of eastern hardwood. The wheel spokes were double-ringed with heavy iron, as were the sixteen-inch hardwood hubs. Heavy wooden axles had a twelve-inch cotter key at the ends. Such relics should have found a new home at the Mono County Museum when Crestview was razed in recent years; however, they were moved to Arizona. According to old-timers, Big Wheels were used at Mono Mills, at a sawmill near Deadman, and at Mammoth.

The center of logging activity for the Hess Mill was the drainage area from the mill north, about two miles. Today the cut-off road to Highway 395 traverses this area; many standing stumps remain. Fifteen to twenty men were employed altogether, and the finished lumber was delivered

 LOGGING WITH HORSE POWER. Frank Huckaby and Ed Dehy loading logs onto a wagon with team and cable, upper photo. *Florence (Huckaby) Smith Collection.* Mule team pulling into a loading area, lower photo. *Art Hess Collection.*

☝ **THE HESS SAWMILL,** 1920 to 1930, in the Jeffrey pine forest beyond Shady Rest Campground. The Hess mill supplied lumber to Old Mammoth as well as June Lake. The forest of tall Jeffrey pine between Mammoth and Mono Lake has been the source of fuel and lumber since the earliest mining days. *Art Hess Collection.*

✍ **BIG WHEELS** (go-devils), particularly useful in hauling heavy logs from rough areas. As pictured above, the driver rode the wheel horse. *H. W. Mendenhall Photo.*

Hauling Logs to Mammoth Sawmill
H.W.M.684

around Mammoth and to June Lake. In 1926 a bad fire leveled the mill buildings. They were rebuilt and the business continued, the output as before. Brother Fred passed away in '29 and it became difficult for the other partner to continue alone. Along in 1930, Arthur dismantled the mill and moved to Bishop, where he now lives. The Inyo Lumber Company, owned by William I. Moffett, continued some work at the site, eventually establishing headquarters at Pleasant Valley, near Bishop.

CAMPING OLD MAMMOTH STYLE.

Family camping in Old Mammoth before there were many cabins or improvements was a happy time. Camps were set up along the creek or in the beautiful forest. During summer vacation many Bishop families sent their children to Mammoth to escape the heat in the valley for the coolness of the mountains and the fun of living outdoors. It was a wonderful way to spend their out-of-school time, usually in the charge of an aunt or perhaps grandparents. There were hikes up the steep, winding road to the lakes or, better, along trails. There was fishing and exploring the old mine sites. A visit to the Summers Store was an event, for Fred Brooks always managed to slip a surprise in each bag of cookies or peanuts. He was loved by all, young and old. Girls as well as women dressed in heavy shirts, knicker pants (the kind that widened above the knees), and high-topped boots.

EARLY CABIN OWNERS.

Two couples, the Barkers and the Carters, residents of Los Angeles, began hearing glowing descriptions of a mountain country beyond the Owens Valley called Mammoth. To them it was a mountain paradise far away across strange country where one would find peace and freedom to camp and fish in lake or stream. They decided to spend a vacation "up there." It was in the year 1914 and travel was not something to be taken lightly. Planning carefully, their camp gear and outfits stowed safely in or on two of those vintage cars, hopefully in sound condition, they were off, in high spirits. It was an adventure!

⌐OLD MAMMOTH STYLE IN THE 1920s. Ruth Hampton and Olive Barker at the Mammoth Store (also known as Summers Store), 1922. They explored much of the magnificent Mammoth country. Their garb was the popular style for hiking—women or girls, locals or tourists. *Olive Barker Collection.*

Malv and Olive Barker drove a one-seater E.M.F. with a White Streak motor. Olive's mother and step-father Sam Carter were driving a Columbia sedan. A minor breakdown in Jawbone Canyon delayed them a little and the sandy tracks up through the desert were slow going. With two overnight camp-outs, they made it to Mammoth in two and one-half days, going up by way of Crooked Creek, their second camp, and skirting Little Round Valley. Olive Barker, who later lived in Bishop, remembered Mammoth this way: "We found a camping spot in a lovely park-like place. The road up through Old Mammoth forked then by the Pelton wheel, coming around the hill through the aspens, and about there we made camp. Pine trees, willows and aspens, wild grass and wild flowers—it was a pleasant spot. We became acquainted with the Ben Williams, camping nearby. There were very few people in the whole area. We spent two seasons there and dreamed of owning a log cabin like the Ben Williams were building. So in 1917 Sam bought some land from Charlie Summers, it was up the road from our camp. He and Malv had logs hauled in, they only cost 50 cents apiece." Ben Williams helped with the building and

⟦63⟧

also John Tibbits and Ed Chamberlain from Bishop. They did much carpenter work around there and lived in their own cabins nearby, in later years. In time, two bedrooms were added to the cabin and also an open-face garage of logs for their cars. The original log cabin was owned for a time by Jim Arness of television fame.

Olive then remarked, "You know, we didn't have much recreation in the early years. Guests came up to visit and we'd all go down to the big corrals just above McGee Creek (near Nan and Max's Long Valley Resort). There we would watch Charlie Summers and his cowboys having a roundup and branding. It was usually a first time for our guests and they loved it. Sometimes we'd drive down to the old swimming hole called Whitmore Springs and enjoy a bath in the warm water. There were no buildings there then, just a widened hole in the meadow and a board gate at the lower end. On our way home, sometimes we would stop at Casa Diablo Hot Springs and show our friends the Indians who camped there." These were mostly Indians who had come over the Fresno Flats Trail from the west side of the Sierra. They loved the steam baths and at first used a wickiup for their baths. Later wooden bath houses were built of Mammoth lumber. The Indian women dressed in bright colors, full-skirted dresses, and colorful head scarves. They were often seen in the woods or along the meadows gathering roots and grasses for basket work, and seeds, pine nuts and piuga for food. (Pronounced pee-ăǵ-gee.) "The piuga (fleshy cater-pillars) were gathered from trenches beneath pine trees in certain areas, steamed in hot earth, then sun dried and stored as a food delicacy for winter use or for trade. Beautiful basketry was brought from the west side for sale or barter. All of this was of great curiosity to visitors."

Mammoth eventually became a permanent home for the Barker family and they had an Indian woman named "Old Nellie" to do their washing and ironing. "She lived on a little place at Whisky Creek near where Crowley Lake is now," Olive remembered, "and she'd come driving in once a week with her horse and buggy. According to custom, she would

☞ THE BEN NOXON FAMILY VACATIONS AT MAMMOTH, 1914. Upper photo, on the road to Mammoth, the Noxons and friends stop to rest at Whisky Creek (south of Hilton Creek). Driving from Los Angeles, they camped out one night on the way. Center photo, camping in the aspens of Old Mammoth. Lower photo, Ben Noxon recalled, "We went camping to Lake Mary for two days. Dad hired a Studebaker Four wagon and four-horse team from Charlie Summers. It was a rough trip." *All photos, Ben Noxon Collection.*

[[64]]

spend the whole day and eat with us at noon. She always came in smiling and greeted us with 'Manahu ta eva wona' (Good morning to everyone)." Nellie used a big iron kettle outdoors over a wood fire to heat water and put out a white-as-snow wash, using tub and washboard. After she passed away her conscientious help was greatly missed. Later in the '40s when they built rental cabins, they named the business Manahu Lodge after their faithful helper.

VALENTINE CAMP.

Tom Williams sold a large acreage in the Mineral Park area to a group of wealthy Los Angeles businessmen in 1915. Early in the '20s they fenced it and with the help of Ed Chamberlain and John Tibbits, the carpenter team from Bishop, built a number of handsome log cabins, including a cook cabin and dining room. Florence Nicoll presided over the dining room and one of the largest of cook stoves for a good many years, while husband Lloyd Nicoll was in charge of maintenance work.

TALES FROM OLD MAMMOTH.

When the Summers Hotel burned, 'tis said every third bucket in the water brigade was full of whiskey! This is how Olive Barker remembered the fire: "It was the winter of 1927 with a foot-or-so of snow on the ground, and

FLORENCE AND LLOYD NICOLL, long-time residents of Old Mammoth. After Lloyd returned from service during World War II, the Nicolls opened Mammoth Lumber and Supply in New Mammoth. *Lloyd Nicoll Collection.*

THE BEN WILLIAMS' CABIN, BUILT IN 1916, one of the first log cabins in Old Mammoth. It still stands, on today's Tamarack Street. *Olive Barker Collection.*

the movie crews were in town. Local people were busy taking care of the extra business. We could hear the commotion. The four of us rushed down to help. Mother grabbed a bottle of whiskey, thinking it might be needed. The flames on the roof were bad and we saw Cece Thorington up there among others. Mother waved the bottle and asked could he use some. 'My God, yes! Send it up in a bucket!' It didn't last long and anyway it was a losing battle, they soon had to leave the roof."

The Boogie Man of Valentine Camp was no myth nor figure of imagination. Pete Christanni, known as "Big Pete" or "Pete the Greek," was a large, burly man with big features. All children gave him a wide path. He was the caretaker of Valentine Camp, which included a sizeable length of Mammoth Creek. Poachers along the creek were bounced by Pete in short order. Children were warned by parents not to stray beyond the fence or "the Boogie Man would get them!" The story of the "bad man" at Valentine persisted long after he'd left the country.

🏚 **EARLY CABIN OWNERS ON THE ROAD TO MAMMOTH, 1914.** Upper photo, driving the long, rough road from Los Angeles, Olive and Malv Barker with her mother and stepfather, Sam Carter. Adventure all the way. Lower photo, Mother and Father Carter and the Barkers at the Wildasinn Store, 1914. Left, the Barkers' one-seater E. M. F. Right, the Carters' Columbia sedan. After camping several summers in Old Mammoth, Sam bought land from Charlie Summers and built a log cabin. *Olive Barker Collection.*

☞ **THE RINCON BARN AND CORRAL ABOVE McGEE CREEK,** the center for Long Valley roundups mentioned by Olive Barker. The "String of Buttons," as cowboys were sometimes called, numbered seventeen. Jim Cline, foreman for the Eaton Land and Cattle Company, at the extreme right. His son is the well-known saddlebronc rider, Lester Cline of Bishop. *H. W. Mendenhall Photo, Les Cline Collection.*

WHITMORE HOT SPRINGS IN THE 1920s, a natural warm water pool and a favorite place to go—Wallace Barker, Lou Stevens, and Malv Barker. In the 1930s it became known as Whitmore Tubs, Helen Eaton, proprietor, advertising tub baths, showers, and an 80-foot pool. *Olive Barker Collection.*

🖐 **THE BEGINNING OF BARKERS' LODGE,** a large log cabin and small tent cabins. The narrow, rough road behind the cabin leads to the Lakes Basin. *Olive Barker Collection.* Lower photo, the lodge in winter. Left to right: the main cabin with living room and kitchen; in back, two bed rooms; a bedroom cabin; the free-for-all bathhouse; garage; another bedroom cabin. It was well known that Sam Carter had the first flush toilet in Mammoth. The property was on the west side of today's Evergreen Street. *Emily (Summers) Foster Collection.*

THE FIRST MAMMOTH GARAGE.

The Mammoth Garage/Shell Service Station was among the first business establishments at Old Mammoth. A friend in the garage where Harold Guseman worked in Los Angeles had been visiting at Mammoth and said, "You should go up there and start a garage, they need one." So it was that, in early spring of 1923, Harold and his father-in-law, Tom Newhall (Gramps), made a trip to Mammoth to look for a possible location for a garage. They were able to drive as far as the flats above Convict Creek, then stalled in ice and snow, as no roads were kept open into the mountains. Not wanting to give up, they decided to hike—quite a problem, as they were dressed in "dude" clothes, low shoes, and thin socks. They made it to the Summers cabin below Laurel Creek and pried open a door. Wood for the stove, ancient coffee in the pot, and stale biscuits saved the day for them. Early the next morning they hiked on up to Mammoth, looked over a lot with cabin on it, across from the Penney Bakery. They had inquired in Bishop at the Forest Service Office about locations. Liking what they found, they returned to Bishop and signed a lease for the lot. The cabin, one story and attic, cost $250.

Their move, with bag and baggage, sounded a bit like *Grapes of Wrath*, as Lil Guseman, long a summer resident, humorously admitted. "Our trip started out good, we had paved road all the way to Mojave. Everything was full to over-flowing. Harold and I and my big black cat sat in the narrow front seat of our old Ford. Gramps was squeezed in the back with his feet on the running board. The little trailer we hauled was piled high, and a fold-up day-bed reposed on top of the Ford. We viewed the rough, dusty tracks with dismay from Mojave on, and sure enough, the trailer tongue broke near Little Lake. Considerable time was lost before we could be on our way. We stopped in Bishop and managed to pack in a few groceries; where, I never will know.

"Near the top of the old grade over Sherwin Hill, our poor old flivver said, 'No more!' Luckily, two young fellows stopped and towed us over the summit. All went well until we neared Mammoth, you remember that last steep little pitch? Well, we had a balky Ford again. The men unloaded, unhitched the trailer and took me to the cabin, where I waited as they went back after our belongings. There I was, perched on top of some stacked lumber. The mice, ugh! They were squeaking and running everywhere in the dark cabin, what a day! That first season Harold managed, with Gramps' help, to build the floor and walls. Then he became so busy on cars, the garage went roofless until the next season. Oh, yes, you asked about shopping in 1923. We could buy a few supplies at Penney's across from us, and there was the Summers Store up on the meadow for more groceries. Had to go to the hotel for milk. I usually took two big two-quart cans, and it cost twenty-five cents for the gallon."

The garage and service station were real necessities. People were moving in and building cabins, and the tourist business was beginning. With long hours and hard labor the Gusemans built a fine business.

FROM BOAT BUILDER TO BAKER.

Frank Penney of Bishop came to Mammoth about 1923 and built himself a small cabin on a Forest Service lease near the Mammoth Creek bridge. He began building boats for some early fishing guides—Ben Williams up at Lake Mary and Nyle Smith at Lake George. Soon the eager fishermen began to ask Frank, "Isn't there someplace we can get sandwiches, a quick lunch to take to the lakes with us?" This prompted the boat builder to cut a window in the front wall of his cabin, put up a shelf, and hang up his sign, "Bakery." He soon had more than he could do and had to bring his wife, Lucy, up from Bishop to help. In time they built a larger "Mammoth Lakes Bakery and Lunch Room"—a busy and popular place.

In the early '30s Frank Jr. and wife Norah Bob took charge of the business. "Bob" (as she became known to friends far and near) baked the best double-sized oatmeal cookies, also bear-claw sweet rolls. The big brick oven in back gave forth the good aroma of homemade bread most hours of the day. Frank managed the front and recalls, "It all kept us too blamed busy, I had no time for my prospecting till late fall!" He has always loved roaming the hills and desert and kept a prospector's pick handy.

FIRST AUTO ROAD TO LAKE MARY, 1920.

The steep, rough wagon road that served the miners of Mammoth City and Pine City (in the general area of today's Old Mammoth Road) remained for many years the only road to the Lakes Basin, adequate for

 HAROLD AND LILLIAN GUSEMAN, in Los Angeles before their move to Mammoth in 1923.

 THE FIRST MAMMOTH GARAGE, established by the Gusemans in Old Mammoth in 1923 and operated by them until they sold to William J. Reed in 1937. The garage was near the Mammoth Creek bridge, opposite Penney's Bakery and Lunch Room. *Both photos, Lil Guseman Collection.*

 Frank Penney's One-Room Cabin, Where He Began A Quick-Lunch Business In 1923 that was an immediate success. In time he and his wife Lucy built a larger bakery and lunch room that was very popular with fishermen and tourists. Right, Frank Jr. and his wife Norah "Bob."

 The Mammoth Lakes Bakery And Lunch Room, near the Mammoth Creek bridge. Frank Jr. and Bob took over the business in the early 1930s, adding fishing tackle and a grocery. Bob's delicious homemade bread, cookies, and pies were a great attraction. *Frank Penney Collection.*

horses but too steep for cars. As more and more automobiles made it to Mammoth, people wanted to drive on farther, all the way to the lakes. Accordingly, construction began on a gentler grade (essentially today's Old Road), as described in this Bishop newspaper:

> LAKE MARY ROAD—The construction on the road from Mammoth to Lake Mary has started and will be finished during the summer. The hard part of this road is about 6000 feet in length but when it is completed it will be a good auto road and will open up one of the most beautiful sections of this country.
>
> The Forest Service has given $4000 for this work and others have donated liberally. Some people here have given as high as $500 and many smaller contributions have been received. Mr. Guy Way, who has charge of the work, is confident that enough money can be raised to put the road in first class shape.
>
> Sometime in August a big barbeque celebration will be given there and everyone interested will be asked to attend and incidentally to furnish a little muscle during the day in helping along this good work. It will only be a question of time until all of the beautiful parts of the High Sierras will be accessible by good auto roads and when that day comes the number of machines that will tour this country in the summertime cannot be estimated. *Owens Valley Herald, July 21, 1920.*

GUIDE SERVICES &
NEW RESORTS ON THE LAKES.

During the 1920s, accomodations and services for guests and fishermen became available on the lakes above Mammoth—several chains of lakes, in all, at the base of Red Mountain and Mammoth Crest. Until 1937, the only route to this lake area was the old mining road to Mammoth City and Pine City. Though greatly improved in 1920, it was still steep and rough.

LAKE GEORGE.

Nyle F. Smith built the first cabin at Lake George, using his big dog to pull timbers and supplies across the ice on a toboggan in winter. In summer boats were (and still are) the only means of transport. A few cabins were built on the lakeshore at the road end. Besides Nyle's boat rentals, there was a campground and Woods Lodge. The rustic lodge overlooking the gem of a lake that mirrors Crystal Crag high above was owned by Ed and Nina Wood.

Nyle And Ruth Smith.

In 1921 Nyle took a Forest Service lease at T. J. Lake for a boat concession and guide service. Besides their Lake George headquarters, "Hill Billy" Smith and his wife Ruth rented boats on Pika, Crystal, and Barrett Lakes. They also began a guide service at Duck Lake, the beautiful high lake that could be reached only by a well-worn pack trail over Duck Pass. They advertised in a brochure titled "Mammoth Lakes in The High Sierras":

> Duck Lake—home of the largest golden trout in the world. We teach you to fish and furnish tackle. Dependable guides.

Nyle held an office in the Eastern Sierra Ski Club, helped pioneer skiing in Mono County, operated a lift one season above Mammoth, and was active in the Mammoth Mountain Ski Club. He and Ruth spent winters in their cabin at Lake George, sometimes skiing down to Penney's Tavern where they joined in the meetings, parties, and visiting. One of the trips was during a bad blizzard. Ruth missed the trail and landed in a hole in the snow around a tree. By the time Nyle missed her, their little dog's barking brought him to the rescue.

In about 1947 the Smiths closed out most of their mountain businesses and bought the buildings on lease property from William Patterson near McGee Creek Lodge on Highway 395, known as Pete Steffens Fox Farm. He had had a good business going, but when the ski lift started up nearby, he had to sell his fox business as the noise spooked his animals. Nyle and Ruth named their place Crowly Lake Resort and had several rental cabins for hunters and fishermen. "Hill Billy" Nyle operated a guide service that was very popular into the 1950s.

Lake Mary.

Lizzie Hammarborg, who had operated a cafe in the boom days at Goldfield, came to Mammoth with her son, John, in 1925. She located

Lake Mary, The Largest Of The Many Lakes In The Lakes Basin. Crystal Crag and Mammoth Crest in the distance. *Stephen Willard Photo.*

near the edge of Lake Mary, where she built the first tent houses as rentals for fishermen. Her fine cooking became widely known, and business was good. A year or so later Barney Johnson of Bishop went into partnership with them and eventually bought their share. The lodge he built nearby, overlooking Lake Mary, he named Crystal Crag for the jagged, pointed spire above. Barney gradually replaced the tent houses with comfortable cabins. He was well liked and the business prospered. He kept several large sled dogs as a hobby. Son Eddie wintered in at the resort several seasons; the sled dogs were his transportation. After he retired there were several changes in ownership. Don Camphouse was one of the later owners.

Lake Mary Store (east of the Lodge) was carpentered by Doc Spencer for owner Jim Gruell in '30 or '31. It became popular with residents and campers. Dwight Defty and wife continued the business for some years.

In the fall of 1923 five acres were designated for a resort high above Twin
Lakes, near the outlet of Lake Mamie. It was a splendid, primeval forest
spot sheltered by a stand of large pines. The lovely-sounding name that
Robert and Hazel Miller chose was "Wildyrie"—meaning "Eagle's Nest."
Most suitable, this Scottish contraction of the two words, *wild* and *eyrie*.
As young Bob remembered, "Mom says she read about the use of the name
in a novel and immediately wanted it for their new project!" The Millers
began building eight cabin shells. In the spring of '24 they were completed
and open for business. During that season they converted one of the
cabins to a general store, known thereafter as "store cabin." Hazel soon

TWIN LAKES, THE LOWEST LAKES IN THE LAKES BASIN. Looking northeast from the top of the
waterfall at the outlet of Lake Mamie. The bridge, built in 1927 by Roy Boothe, H. H. Simpson,
Bill Reed, and Guy Way, brought campers and cabin owners into the pretty, forested area on the
lakes' west shore. *Stephen Willard Photo.*

initiated a big attraction! Seven days a week she baked bread and homemade pies (eleven loaves one day, twenty-two the next). Oh, that fresh bread aroma! Soon a larger building housed the store, a dining room, and a post office. R. F. Miller became postmaster in 1934 of the first post office above Old Mammoth (4th class). A service station was added and the cabins increased to 20.

Along in 1937 the new highway to Horseshoe Lake cut the original site in half. The buildings had to be moved to the hillside above the east shore of Lake Mamie. A new lodge with upstairs living quarters was built near the entrance to the new site. Sons Robert and Harry and daughter Sybil helped carry on until they sold in 1944. The resort was known for a time as White's Lodge, but later was re-named Wildyrie.

TWIN LAKES.

Another woman established a resort at the edge of beautiful Twin Lakes. Mary Foy, daughter of a famous pioneer Los Angeles family, built the first Tamarack Lodge and operated it for fishermen in the early '20s. Mr. and Mrs. Lloyd Austin bought the lodge in 1927 and remodeled it some years later. With Lloyd's background (Switzer's at Arroyo Seco in the Sierra Madre), it wasn't long until he'd added a spacious dining room and began nightly programs for their guests.

Beatrice Willard advised, "No single person did more for Mammoth than our neighbor, Lloyd B., along the line of promotion of the natural beauty and interest. At his own expense, he had trails built to many points of importance and even a trail to the top of Mt. Mammoth. His advice to all, 'Get all you can of our good outdoors—hike, see and enjoy.' " The rustic log chapel across the narrows of Twin Lakes was built by the Austins. It was there daughter Alice and Don McGuffin were married. Mammoth residents gathered at the lodge for the happy event. Don and Alice were escorted down the hill and across the little foot bridge by a large group singing "For Me and My Gal." Wildflowers in profusion graced the picturesque chapel and Alice carried a large colorful bouquet.

Jim Gruell and Morrell Austin, son of Lloyd and Bertha, established the Twin Lakes Store and Service Station. Later, Morrell bought his partner's interest and continued as manager.

THE WILLARD STUDIO.

There is still a rustic little studio in a lovely alpine setting just opposite the upper road into Twin Lakes. For over fifty years, gracious Beatrice Willard greeted all who came to her door with a smile and a welcome. This was one business that remained in the same ownership, true to tradition of old, through the 1970s. The front yard is still filled with the beauty and color of wildflowers. The large studio window framed one of Stephen Willard's pictures on an easel—a lake, mountain peaks, scenes from remote areas, always something outstanding. Until his death in 1966, Steve worked endlessly to capture unusual, unique beauty and transfer it to paper and canvas for others to enjoy.

The Willards owned a little studio in Palm Springs when that city had only sandy streets. Setting out to find a summer location they searched several mountain areas only to return to the first they visited. "We fell in love with Mammoth," Beatrice mentioned. "We contacted the Forest Service Ranger and he located us on a nice spot near the top of the Mammoth City road, the original road to the lakes. It was in the year 1924 that we moved in and we worked very hard and long hours, Steve and I, to build a tiny studio and living quarters. We didn't have much, but managed to get along by doing most of our own work, even to photo-finishing in those first years. Wanting something rustic in our studio in keeping with the rugged outdoors, we had pine slabs with the bark on brought up from the Hess Sawmill." Sales counter, benches, shelves, and trim all still show the crude, textured beauty of aged pine bark.

"About two years after we'd built, along came a small but seemingly serious happening. A very upset mining man came and told us we had built on his mining claim! We were very worried. Steve went to the Forest Service and they checked over all the records. Well, you see they found the man's claim was not that far down on Red Mountain, so we were all right, after all. My! but that was a worry for a time!"

In 1934 they were given notice they would have to move up on the new highway being built to the lakes. "Roy Boothe, Supervisor on the Inyo, was so kind and thoughtful, he had a perfect spot surveyed for us, a sheltered area in the pines well above the road where it is never very windy. Here we've been ever since, and we raised our daughter here." The Studio was more than just a business to the Willards, more like having a

 STEPHEN WILLARD, MAMMOTH PHOTOGRAPHER AND PAINTER FOR OVER FORTY YEARS, changing a tire (36 × 4) on his 1909 Chalmers Detroit. He used this car to explore the desert while he lived in Palm Springs. After he gave it to Harold Guseman, Mammoth Garage, Harold used it as a tow-car, the first in Old Mammoth. *Stephen Willard Photo.*

big family, as people and friends returned every year, if only to chat awhile. Their aim, always, was to encourage visitors to see all the points of interest and to know the history and tradition that is Mammoth.

Through the 1920s Stephen owned an old car, a 1909 Chalmers Detroit, the forerunner of the Chalmers cars. As a hobby he made trips, sometimes where there were no roads, accompanied by a friend, testing the roadability of the different tire sizes. In later years he gave the old car to his war-time buddy, Harold Guseman. It became the first tow-car in Old Mammoth.

TAMARACK LODGE-MAMMOTH LAKES, CALIFORNIA

✍ **TRAIL SIGN IN THE LAKES BASIN, 1922,** at the forks of Lake Mary Road. Grace and Tim Stephens discovered it while vacationing at the Summers Hotel. *Grace Stephens Collection.*

NEW RESORTS ON THE LAKES, built in the early 1920s. Below, Wildyrie Store and Dining Room, near the outlet of Lake Mamie. *Stephen Willard Photo, R. W. Miller Collection.* Opposite page, above, Tamarack Lodge at Twin Lakes. *Stephen Willard Photo.* Opposite page, below, the Willards' Mammoth Lakes Studio, up the road from Twin Lakes. Their Pierce Arrow sedan parked at the side. *Stephen Willard Photo.*

 TWIN LAKES IN WINTER, Crystal Crag and Mammoth Crest in the distance. The foot bridge leads from Tamarack Lodge to the rustic Forest Chapel. *Harry Prier Collection.*

 ABOVE THE ALTAR OF THE FOREST CHAPEL Lloyd Austin placed these words, "I will lift up mine eyes unto the hills." *Stephen Willard Photo.*

HARRY PRIER,
WINTER CARETAKER,
REMINISCES.

Among those who worked as caretakers at the lake resorts, which were snowbound in winter, were: Al Van Horn, George Cook, Harry Prier, Doc Spencer, Lynn Phelps, Elmer and Vi Cannon, Mr. and Mrs. Allen Purcell, Rick Grodon, Melvin Spaethe, Nan and Max Zischank, and Dick and Sybil Rogers. In 1941 Collins and Warren were operating the Monte Cristo Mine above Lake Mary. Art Kniefelcamp worked there and also wintered in during the operation (a few short years).

Harry Prier recalled his introduction to the superb high lakes country and his years at Tamarack Lodge. "In 1931 I left Los Angeles by train to Mojave. There I transferred to the narrow-gauge train to Lone Pine, then by bus to Bishop for overnight. From there Gus Alexander, deliveryman into Mono County, took me by truck to Camp Hi-Sierra where I enjoyed my two-week vacation. That was the beginning. I became an employee the year around at Tamarack Lodge in the '30s and they were the most gratifying years. I was winter caretaker and in summer 'jack of all trades'. The first road to Tamarack, by way of Mammoth City mining camp, went down past the Twin Lakes Store, Tamarack Lodge, and private cabins and ended at the outlet of the lower lake. This was the beginning of Mammoth Creek and the take-off of the historic covered ditch that ran around Panorama Dome to the mines. The hike following the ditch was always a favorite of mine. We summer employees at Tamarack numbered twenty or so; the number of guest cabins had grown. We became known as 'The Bears' and used a private dining room. We were happy workers.

"In winter the caretakers at lodges around the lakes sometimes visited back and forth, when we could, for a little recreation. At times our visits were far between, in that huge white world around each of us. One winter we counted but thirteen people living 'up the hill'.

"Skating while the ice lasted and skiing near Lake Mary was great. On January 17, 1940, we gathered with friends from Mammoth and skied, and/or skated, sang songs, ate and had a generally good visit. We called the group charter members in the *Glee and Ski Club of Mammoth Lakes*. It turned out to be only a one-season thing. The next winter Uncle Sam and World War Two called several of us."

Bertha Austin died in 1942 and during the next few years Lloyd B. began to weaken. Don and Alice McGuffin took over the management of the lodge until their retirement. Pasted in one of Harry's albums we found the following:

WHY VISIT TAMARACK THIS YEAR, 1938?
Because the very heavy snowfall of the past winter means the grandest scenic effects of a lifetime in roaring waterfalls, brimming lakes and streams, summer snowfields and flower strewn meadows.

ICE HARVEST.

In the '20s and '30s, business people depended on ice gathered from Twin Lakes for the following summer tourist season. It was imperative that the cutting and storing of the ice chunks be completed at just the right time, usually late fall, before the ice was ruined by rain or snow.

Harry Prier vividly described the ice harvest: "Working for the Lloyd B. Austins was good work and sometimes hard work, as the cutting of ice each fall for storage. Several workers were needed to get the job done. It

THE GLEE AND SKI CLUB—left to right, unknown, Jim and Jo Wallace, Dick and Sybil Rogers, Elmer and Vi Cannon, Jerry Packard at Twin Lakes. January, 1940. *G. A. Packard Collection.*

CUTTING ICE ON TWIN LAKES, Doc Spencer and Tex Cushion. *Stephen Willard Photo.*

was a race with the weather as the ice had to be a certain thickness. In 1937 we worked December 4, 5, 6 and 7th. Morrell Austin, Fred Sanson, Paul Yates and myself made the crew. We were paid $8 per day. Regular two-man saws were used with one handle removed. The Tamarack truck hauled to a well-insulated building that Morrell had built not far from the Chapel foot bridge.

"Morrell sold ice at his Twin Lakes store. At Tamarack it was mainly used for packing fish for their guests. Other businesses cut their own ice, as at Lake Mary where they sold it. Frank Penney built his ice house near the lower end of Twin Lakes. He usually brought up a crew from Old Mammoth for the cutting and storage." Jim and Jo Wallace also cut and hauled ice from Twin Lakes to their ice house on Old Mammoth Road near the Mammoth Garage.

🖑 HARVESTING ICE AT TWIN LAKES FOR THE AUSTINS' ICE HOUSE. Loading ice chunks onto the Tamarack truck, which was driven as close as possible to the edge of the ice.

🖎 STORING ICE IN THE AUSTINS' ICE HOUSE AT TWIN LAKES IN LATE FALL, to supply Tamarack Lodge and the Twin Lakes Store the following summer. Dick Rogers on the right. The walls of the ice house were filled with sawdust from the Hess Sawmill in Mammoth. Sawdust between the chunks provided additional insulation.

☞ HARRY PRIER, CARETAKER AT TAMARACK LODGE IN THE 1930S. One of Harry's jobs was to gather crews each fall to harvest ice. *All photos, Harry Prier Collection.*

✍ CREW HARVESTING ICE: Nyle Smith and George Ace, left; Dick Rogers, far right.

DAIRIES IN THE MEADOWS.

Mammoth people did not have a bank or a drug store, and many other services were missing in the '20s and '30s, but dairies they did have and good fresh, whole milk. The Summers family kept a few cows on the meadow and sold the milk at the hotel. Alvie Bodle had bought the meadowland known as Windy Flat from Tom Williams and built a log cabin near the Nadeau cabin. (The location of both is best described today as being just back of the Arcularius home, left of the Old Mammoth Road.) The lower end of Windy Flat soon became known as Bodle Meadow and supported a small herd of milk cows. Alvie delivered milk to residents and to the hotel.

Another herd of milk cows (Holsteins) were moved up from Bishop in the early '20s; the A. W. Wonacotts, Bob and Carrie and their family, moved into the old Summers cabin at Laurel. In exchange for use of the

 HERD OF MILK COWS, BODLE MEADOW, lower end of Windy Flat. *Stephen Willard Photo.*

◁ **BOB WONACOTT, OUR CHEER-FUL MILKMAN, AND HIS WIFE CARRIE,** long-time dairy owners in both Inyo and Mono counties. They grazed their herd in the meadows along Laurel Creek. Later on they moved to Hot Creek and pastured them in meadows there. *Carrie Wonacott Collection.*

pastures, Bob took care of the Summers' cows with his own and delivered milk to the hotel. Sometime later the Wonacott Dairy moved to the Jim Watterson property at Hot Creek. The family lived in a cabin just above the meadow. They established a retail route for delivering milk to all the campgrounds at Mammoth and in the Lakes Basin, north to Crestview, and south to Convict Lake and Rock Creek Lodge. When the City of Los Angeles was building the Crowley Lake dam, they delivered milk to the work camp. Throughout our camping years at Mammoth, Bob was our cheerful milkman. He could be depended on for a smile, a greeting, a joke, and a bit of news.

PACK OUTFITS.

Riding the high trails is an exciting adventure. One becomes a single unit in the packer's string, all tensions of the work-a-day world fading away, an entirely different world unfolding. Dim forest trails with perhaps bear tracks and animal scent to spook your horse. High rocky passes where the

 PACK TRAIN AT DUCK LAKE, on the trail to Cascade Valley. *Stephen Willard Photo.*

vegetation and bright flowers are mini-size and the views of peaks and lakes superb. Steep hairpin trails that drop down into lush meadows circled with aspen and willow, a deer showing now and then. And best of all, the night camps—a hearty camp supper followed by a social hour around a blazing log fire. It is then that a sleeping bag feels like a bed fit for a king. Wake-up time and the aroma of breakfast, on the edge of a white-frosted meadow, is something very special!

The first pack strings worked out of Old Mammoth from the big barn and corrals. Cece Thorington was packer for a time, then he began his own camp at McGee Creek. The Summers family (sons and grandsons of Charlie) continued in the packing business. Lee Summers tells of his first days taking tourists over the trails. "We used to follow the old trail from the corrals up and over the summit (Fresno Flats Trail) and usually packed the High Trail all the way to Thousand Island Lake and the upper San Joaquin area." He grinned as he mentioned, "It was a long haul in those days but the people all liked it. There was never a complaint." Through the years Mammoth Pack had several locations—back of the sawmill on the meadow, across from Tex Cushion's Winter Patrol, and in the meadow across Lake Mary where Fred Hamer was in charge. Then their headquarters were on the edge of old Pine City across from the present pack camp, with Lloyd and Sybil in charge. After Lee's stint in the army in Alaska, he returned to Mammoth Pack, continuing the business after Lloyd's passing until he sold in the '60s.

Another pack camp in charge of Charlie Roberts operated in 1927 below Lake Mary on the little creek. He sold to Don McGuffin and Ed Brown, Don later buying out his partner. Packers experienced many humorous incidents in their daily work. Don McGuffin was one who enjoyed relating these tales to guests around a big campfire at headquarters. The most unusual he told was about packing a couple into Cascade Valley and down the rugged trail to Fish Creek Hot Springs. The springs were a "must" for all trips in the area; the warm mineral water was very welcome and relaxing. Small, wide holes in the little meadow stream were hidden back of clumps of willow, and one could soak away the dust and sore muscles. This camp was usually a one-night stop, but this time the birth of a lusty baby, with Don acting as midwife, changed all plans.

◈ **LLOYD SUMMERS AT THE MAMMOTH PACK CAMP.** He and his wife Sybil had their headquarters at the edge of old Pine City, at the base of Red Mountain. Later they moved their cabins, corrals, and stock across to the present camp.

Several generations of the Summers family have owned and operated pack camps. The first pack strings worked out of the big barn and corrals in Old Mammoth. In 1932 Lloyd Summers started a pack camp at Reds Meadow. Charlie Jr. and his wife Altha ran a camp at Agnew Meadow. Then Lloyd and Sybil managed Mammoth Pack Camp for a number of years. Their son Lee continued the business into the 1960s. *Verne Summers Collection.*

 Sybil (McGee) Summers And Packer Dave Jackson. Sybil and Lloyd Summers operated Mammoth Pack Camp. She was also known and loved as Mammoth's Smiling Postmistress. Dave, 98 years young in this photo, was one of the first packers in Mammoth. *Verne Summers Collection.*

Don always mentioned, "She told me she had a tumor! Well, it meant we had to stay in camp a few days, then head back to Mammoth."

In 1932 Lloyd Summers started a pack camp at Reds Meadow, an ideal location for starting off on pack trips into the primitive back country and also along the old Fresno Flats Trail. Archie and Gladys Mahan took it over, built a store and cabins, and operated it for many years. After selling the resort, Arch and Gladys built a home in Mammoth and lived there year round.

Charlie and Altha Summers, with their children Jack and Emily, operated a pack camp at Agnew Meadow. A nearby campground accommodated hikers and riders. From Agnew Meadow they packed into Thousand Island Lake, Shadow Lake, Lake Ediza, and numerous other lakes and streams at the headwaters of the San Joaquin. Of all our activities, we felt riding the high trails to be "one of the greatest." We enjoyed many of the trails out of Mammoth during our years there.

New Lodge In Old Mammoth.

Woodmen of the World Lodge of Bishop purchased several acres in the attractive, timbered Mineral Park area. They used the site mainly for summer picnics, get-togethers for members' families, and sometimes an outdoor initiation. Along in the mid-twenties the property was sold to Lem and Mary (Auntie May) Gish and her sister, Julia Rogers. The Gishes were long-time residents of Laws, near Bishop. They had moved to the Owens Valley from San Jose by wagon and team via the Greenhorn Mountains in the 1890s. Lem, a descendant of the Donner party pioneers, became a prominent rancher before moving to Mammoth. Julia Rogers, widowed, came to Laws in 1907 with two children, Buck and Naomi. She sold her store there and became half-owner of the Pine Cliff Lodge and cabins the three built in Mineral Park. Their lodge was southwest of the road to the lakes, near the foot of the Mill City grade. Son Buck spent the summer of '26 helping to wire the lodge and cabins for a Kohler light plant. These plants were gradually installed in all resorts and businesses; a few used Diesel plants. These were a great luxury item—no more lamps and gasoline lanterns to care for. After Julia Rogers' death the Gishes continued to manage Pine Cliff Camp until retirement.

On The Way To Pine Cliff Camp In Winter. Co-owners Mary Gish and Julia Rogers ride behind Tex's dog team. *Olive Barker Collection.*

[95]

THE MAMMOTH DOG TEAMS:
FREIGHT & PASSENGER SERVICE.

Tex Couchane (or Cushion), a French Canadian, and his wife Ruth arrived in Old Mammoth the winter of 1927. They acquired a dog team, which supplied winter transportation—a way in and out for this snow-bound community where a handful of people lived far from the "outside." No snowplow or snow-go cleared roads in those days.

Each winter Tex and his dogs reigned supreme over a wide expanse of white country. During blizzards the snow drifted and concealed roads and tracks with a white blanket. Nothing looked familiar. Other times it was icy or powdery or so bottomless even the dogs had to "hole up." Yet, somehow, Tex and his team maintained a regular patrol to caretakers' cabins around the lakes, carrying supplies and mail. They also freighted to a mine many rugged miles beyond the Summit; the Minaret Mine was able to operate in winter only because of the dogs! Tex recalled, "On one trip to the mine I used twenty-three dogs and hauled 1500 pounds of mine equipment. It was a long, hard pull. Sometimes a blizzard would catch us near the Summit. I would shovel down, find a window at the old Starkweather cabin. We'd all climb down into the cabin for shelter. When on long trips, I sometimes used two sleds and the twenty-three dogs. My lead dog was 94 feet beyond me, yet worked perfectly by normal tone, voice command. For a fast run, necessary at times, my order was, 'Load lite, bind tite, and go like hell!' "

The Cushions gradually imported and trained younger dogs for replacement. They also raised Malamute pups. Tex claimed one dog, Sergeant, was "the meanest and most ornery dog I ever trained, but turned out to be the best worker in the whole outfit." Their Winter Patrol cabin was south of the road after leaving Windy Flat. The dog kennels and high wire pens were just across the road. Tex depended on one or more regular helpers who lived and boarded with them. Removing snow from summer cabins was another chore, part of the business. Coley Ward was a long time, regular helper. Russell Howard, Fred Sanson, Carl Grebe, and "little" Dutch Spaethe each worked there at times. For many winters the teams and drivers worked with movie crews who found Mammoth an ideal location for snow scenery.

 Tex Cushion And Team In Long Valley. Perhaps on location with the movies.

Each spring Tex hauled teams and gear to the Automobile Club's Outing Show in Los Angeles. The famed driver, his dogs, pups, and sleds attracted much interest. The change from snow country to sunny southern California was difficult for the dogs; ice chunks in the pens helped.

On one of my visits with Tex, he began to chuckle and asked, "Did you know I used to run a saloon in the liquor store in Old Mammoth? It was in 1931 and I called it, 'The Biggest Little Saloon in All the World.' I will tell you a story and it's a true one. The crew working on the new Mammoth Lakes highway used to depend on me to cash checks, so I kept a good amount of cash on hand. The City Tunnel Camp also had a big payroll to meet. They got a tip that the gangster, 'Pretty Boy' Floyd, was about to pay us a visit and sent me word. I put Coley Ward behind a barricade in the Sierra Cafe with a rifle. I checked my six-gun. Two Texas boys at the gaming table stepped up to side me. Excitement, wow! As we watched, a limousine was rolling slowly up the street. They suddenly quickened speed, made a turn at the Pelton wheel, and came roaring down past us lickety split! Must have smelled a rat, I always figured!"

Nan and Max Zischank, close friends of the Cushions, have added the following details to memories of the dog-team days at Mammoth. Feeding the Malamutes and pups at headquarters, as well as the extra dogs kept in a high-wire pen below Laurel Creek at the Summers place, meant a lot of work. Two kinds of food were necessary: raw meat for the winter work season, a lighter diet for summer. Through the winter, when the roads were open, Tex and one of his mushers would drive to Bishop for dog food. Farmers would send word of dead animals to be butchered. During the heavy snow of 1933 at Bishop, when many animals were marooned far out in fields, he brought along the dogs and sled. The cuts of meat were stored in the meat house back of the dog pens in Old Mammoth. Here a large iron vat was set up on a stone foundation with space under the vat for a wood fire. Cracklings and scraps from the Charles Matlick Slaughter House near Bishop were mixed with cornmeal and cooked. After cooling, the mixture was cut into three-pound chunks—one to a dog in summer. It was also trail food to take along when needed. The kettle was in use for years, then one night the roof leaked in a storm, the water froze and cracked it. The vat made a fine wood-box at the Long Valley Resort.

At feeding time the dogs had to be chained separately to the fence to prevent fighting. When the snow got to the top of the nine-foot fence,

Tex With "Dawson." *Unless noted otherwise, all dog team photos are from Tex Cushion's Collection.*

[98]

they were chained at all times. If they had a chance, they would fight to the death over a bone. At such times Tex had to use his bull whip. It was great fun to watch the fat, roly-poly pups when meat and bones were thrown in their pen—wild scuffling and growling, with usually the largest pup cornering the largest bones. When old enough to follow the sled team to Penney's Tavern, the pups frolicked along. While the team curled up in the snow waiting for Tex, the youngsters scouted all over the area. It was startling to see their faces lined up and pressed against a window partly covered with snow. Ears up, curious, then away they scampered.

Nan Zischank recalls, "One day Tex answered the telephone and it was Barney Johnson of Crystal Crag. He said, 'My dog team will be coming down the trail past you in about five minutes. Please stop the so and so's! I harnessed them and forgot to hook to the sled. When I yelled "Mush" they took off and there I stood on the sled.' Sure enough they made it on time and Tex corraled them."

During Old Mammoth days, Tex and his dogs were always on call for emergencies. Also, during the first years that New Mammoth was building, he was called on to help in times of heavy snow. He would take the sick or the injured by sled to wherever Highway 395 was open or to the top of Sherwin Grade where a doctor from Bishop would meet them.

Tex claims Malamutes are most affectionate. This poem, from his photo album, expresses his feelings for them:

You can't tell me God would have Heaven
So a man couldn't mix with his friends;
That we're doomed to meet disappointment
When we come to the place the trail ends.
That would be a low-grade sort of Heaven,
And I'd never regret a damned sin
If I mush up to the Gates, white and pearly,
And they don't let my Malamute in.

For I know it would never seem homelike,
No matter how golden the strand
If I lose out that pal-loving feeling
Of a Malamute's nose in my hand.

—*Author Unknown*

 THE "MEAT HOUSE," WHERE DOG FOOD WAS STORED AND PREPARED, adjacent to the high-fenced dog pens. Carl Grebe, musher, in the doorway. *Harry Prier Collection.*

 RUTH CUSHION TRAINING YOUNG DOGS. She also boarded the "mushers" (helpers).

👆 **WINTER PATROL HEADQUARTERS AND THE DOG PENS IN WINTER,** across the road from each other in Old Mammoth. Tex and Ruth lived in the Patrol cabin. The mushers lived in the tent houses. Having the dogs available for winter emergencies and transportation made all the difference to the people of Old Mammoth. Lower photo: pups, always alert and curious.

☞ **Two Teams Resting At Minaret Summit.** En route to the Minaret Mine, west of the San Joaquin River and far up Minaret Creek canyon. In winter, the miners depended on the dogs for mail, supplies, and transportation.

☞ **Buildings Of The Minaret Mine,** which operated from 1928 to 1930. On one long, hard trip Tex hauled 1500 pounds of mine equipment, using two sleds and 23 dogs. The dog teams made regular runs to the mine.

☞ **Dog Team Heading Across Lake Mary.** Teams brought mail, newspapers, medicine, and supplies of all kinds to snowbound miners and caretakers. Tex had wonderful control over his dogs.

PLAY BALL, 1928.

A ball team was organized the summer of 1928, mostly Forest Service and sawmill employees. Mina, Nevada, sent a challenge, a date was set, and players, wives, gals and friends set out one Saturday afternoon in July. It was dusty going, by way of Benton Crossing, Wild Rose Grade, Old Benton, and the long pull to Summit House at Montgomery Pass. On the way we were not allowed to forget that we had a snappy leader. Les Altis, the team's captain, was driving a new, fancy sports car, with shining trim and accessories. He put his 1928 Auburn through its antics, revving up the powerful motor, then off he'd go, far in the lead. We were bringing up the rear in a '26 Essex sedan, quite a "hotrod" itself. Leaving the pass, we soon turned off the Tonopah road and followed tracks and cow trails, in and out of many gullies and dips, each with a washout in the bottom. We bounced along at a slow pace. The comforts offered at the two-story Baker Hotel in Mina that evening were very welcome.

About mid-day Sunday the game began on a flat, glaring dry lake-bed. The sun beat down in full force. The faces of onlookers who crowded close to the diamond were filled with stirring enthusiasm! The chatter of the players, the cheering and/or booing of the crowd echoed across to the desert hills. Undertones were the clink of silver dollars changing hands. Cigar smoke wafted through the air, and liquid refreshments made the rounds. In a very exciting game, the desert team put up a good fight but

THE SAWMILL BASEBALL TEAM, 1928. Bill Reed and Tex Cushion, right. *Adele Reed Photo.*

the mountain boys did a little better. In high spirits, we began the homeward trek. True to his promise, Les Altis hosted a fine chicken dinner at Summit House—for all. A weary but happy group pulled into Mammoth later that evening. It had been a big event!

SUMMERS STORE BECOMES LUTZ GROCERY.

Del Lutz, a grocer in Bishop, came to Mammoth in 1933 and took over the Summers Store. When he passed away in early 1934, son John and his wife Laura (Keough) moved to Mammoth and continued the Lutz Grocery. They lived in one of the little cabins built by Charles Summers in back of the Pelton wheel. John and Laura would go down to the store to open up early each morning. John soon had a roaring fire in the long cast-iron heater. Soon Big Pete or Bud Davis would stop in, to sit on one of the long benches beside the stove and talk awhile. Bud was in charge of the Standard Station across the road. Big Pete worked at Valentine Camp.

OUR VILLAGE IN THE 1930s.

Our village in the meadow straddled the old road as shown in the photo section. During our summers in the high country, this was "our town." The Standard Service Station on the left, owned by Sam and Lilas Griffith of Bishop and operated by Bud Davis, boasted two visible gas pumps. The next building was first a Trading Post, where Navajo Johnson sold Indian handcrafts and turquoise jewelry. Then it became the Mammoth Liquor Store with Bill Treglown as manager. Later, as the Mammoth Saloon, true stories told of weird patterns in the ceiling made by six-guns.

The Lutz Grocery on the right, formerly Summers Store, was a typical "mercantile" of days past. One could find most anything needed or something that would do as well. It also dispensed kerosene for lamps and white gas for the more popular gasoline lanterns. Left of the store was the Sierra Cafe, operated by Nellie N. Coe. The cook, Jay Tyler, became quite famous for his high-standing lemon meringue pies. After the hotel burned, this building became our community gathering place. With tables and chairs stacked in one corner and wax on the floor, residents would gather for a party. Sometimes it was used for important meetings and once for a wedding. It was also the scene of the first Catholic services held in

 Sheep on Bodle Meadow, a common sight in Old Mammoth. *Laura (Keough) Lutz Collection.*

Old Mammoth, when Father Maginnis came from Lee Vining and sent out a call for the needed number, 25 or more. Left of the cafe in the distance stands the great rock fireplace alone in the meadow, a mute reminder of Mammoth Camp.

Our road into Mammoth turned off of Highway 395 below Casa Diablo, a little beyond the Mammoth Creek bridge. It angled across the meadow near the Standard Oil Plant and up a steep switchback. It then was mostly in sight of Mammoth Creek and the camping spots, ending at the garage and the bakery.

CASA DIABLO HOT SPRINGS.

Nothing at all remains of the historic hot-water spa known as Casa Diablo. The steam vents, warm springs here and there, and small streams have mostly disappeared. But in the old days the springs were popular for hot baths. The Indians took their soakings inside wickiups set over a spring. Later, small buildings made of Mammoth lumber enclosed "baths." Prospectors and travelers found here a welcome "rest and relax stop!" The old log cabin was used for a time as a supply store, then as an Indian Trading Post. In the early 1900s, Charlie Summers purchased the forty acres adjacent to the springs from the cattleman, Rawson. They remained in the Summers family for many years. A gas pump and garage service were available at Casa Diablo for a time, since it was on old Highway 395, just north of the Mammoth Lakes turnoff. And for a time Casa Diablo supported a dining room, bar, and dance floor.

The peculiar on-and-off behavior of the Casa Diablo geyser became noticeable after a well-drilling attempt, which failed to produce more than a small stream of hot water. The geyser, located in a small ravine back of the cafe and bar, would rest for a time then break forth with gusto! In late 1937 it really came alive, spurting hot, steamy water 70 to 80 feet in the air. Against a background of snowy mountains, it was a spectacular sight. It continued for several months, attracting people to look and take photographs. The freezing temperature caused the moisture to coat all nearby objects with ice in a fascinating manner, including the power lines of the Southern Sierras Power Company.

Long Valley Resort.

The Zischanks, Nan and Max, came to Mammoth in the early '30s. After various work they decided to become caretakers, wintering in at Tamarack Lodge on Twin Lakes. Tex Cushion taught them how to manage on skis, and he and Ruth helped them plan for "living in," far from stores and any services. The State was making a big effort to keep Highway 395 open, but there were long periods when nothing was open north of Bishop.

Shortly before Christmas Tex appeared at the lodge with Ruth's welcome invitation, "Come down and help us eat the big turkey I'm roasting." Early Christmas Eve Nan and Max skied down to the Patrol Cabin, they were given the guest tent-house (it had a wood heater). Nan remembers, "We had a lot of fun that evening making popcorn strings for the pretty little tree. We added sparkling bits of jewelry and trinkets. You know, we were all poor together those days and simple things meant a lot." After Christmas dinner they went by dog team to Casa Diablo, then by car to Whitmore Springs to enjoy the warm mineral water. (By this time there were cabins with big cement tubs. The water came in one end and went out the other, a big improvement over the open swimming hole.) The dog team returned them to Old Mammoth, and the notable event of their winter ended wth a long uphill trek on skis.

They lived and worked at Crestview several years, then bought a barracks building at the City Tunnel Camp and had Gert Crawford move

✍ **OLD LOG CABIN AT CASA DIABLO HOT SPRINGS,** just before it was razed in the 1950s. No one knows how long it stood—through wind, storm, frost and snow. It is widely believed that it was a stage stop in the 1870s on the Bishop Creek–Bodie stage line. *Adele Reed Photo.*

📖 **CASA DIABLO CABIN IN THE 1930S,** housing Navajo Johnson's trading post. *Laura (Keough) Lutz Collection.*

☞ THE CASA DIABLO GEYSER, LATE 1937, spurting hot water 70 to 80 feet in the air. It would rest for a time, then break forth with gusto! It is always possible that some day it may again come alive. *Stephen Willard Photo.*

🖐 CASA DIABLO HOT SPRINGS, long popular for its hot steam baths with whites and Paiutes alike. Bath houses, made of Mammoth lumber, were built on the hillside as well as on the flat below the geyser. See also Mendenhall photo, page 5. *Frasher Collection, Pomona Public Library.*

🖐 WICKIUPS (SWEAT HOUSES) AT CASA DIABLO, 1917. Used by the local Paiutes as well as by Indians from the west side of the Sierra, who followed ancient trails across the mountains in summer to visit and trade. *Oliver Barker Collection.*

☞ Nan And Max Zischank At Their Long Valley Resort. Nan cooked delicious meals, Max was barkeep and man of all trades. *Nan Zischank Collection.*

it to Long Valley. Remodeled, it became the well-known Nan and Max Long Valley Resort and remained in their charge until they retired to Bishop. Today it is a restaurant, the Normandy Inn.

Little George.

George Dahlquist was a long-time familiar figure about Mammoth. His genial, happy manner overcame many problems. He was the unfortunate victim of a buzz saw accident that meant the loss of one leg. He and Harold Guseman were sawing wood the fall of 1934. A faulty mandril

✑Little George Dahlquist, who used three snowshoes when hunting ducks and geese in fall. *Nan Zischank Collection.*

meant a rush trip towards Bishop, with Doc Boody meeting them on Sherwin Hill after Lil's emergency call. The Doc gave him first aid, took him to Bishop, then sent him to Los Angeles by car, where he remained for a year. Bishop had two doctors but no hospital then.

Later, George and his wife, Annie, decided to build their own home near Nan and Max in Long Valley. Every able-bodied person up and down the area closed shop and gave a day's work. A log raising, only it was lumber! The ladies brought an abundance of food. It was a happy, working-together time. George became an avid fisherman, managing his own boat on Crowley Lake. Fall and early winter found him on snowshoes, three of them, eagerly hunting ducks and geese. One snowy day a hunter, rather full-of-firewater, came rushing into Nan and Max exclaiming, "There's a three-legged monster wearing three snowshoes and he has a long tail, I saw him down near the lake!" The so-called tail was his string of ducks, roped to his waist and trailing behind.

RHYS & VIOLET MAY'S GUIDE SERVICE.

Rhys May, grandson of pioneer Alney McGee, could be termed "a chip off the old block." He loves the outdoors and fishing and hunting. He and wife Violet have lived it, just that way. Their hobby became their occupation after they moved into Old Mammoth. Along with fishing and hunting guide service, they began the High Sierra Worm Farm in 1935. Two tent houses connected with a porch between (the deluxe in summer tenting then), located in the timber between Old and New Mammoth, were headquarters. Nearby were the large worm vats. Violet sighed as she mentioned, "Mine was the never ending job of counting worms, thousands of them, into small containers!" They wholesaled them to resorts, from Gene Crosby's Paradise Camp at the foot of Sherwin Grade north to Lee Vining. In those years of the '30s the lakes, streams, and the Owens River teemed with Rainbow and Eastern Brook. Fat, sleek Goldens could be found lurking deep in the highest lakes, wary of most bait.

In wintertime, after the worm vats were covered, the tents folded away, Rhys and Violet trapped for coyotes at Mono Lake, River Springs, Deep Springs, and Fish Lake Valley. The many fine hides were then processed for shipment to the east. The winters of '37 and '38, the Mays

RHYS AND VIOLET MAY, WHO OPENED THE HIGH SIERRA WORM FARM IN 1935. Vi counting some of the jillions of worms they raised, Rhys proving they had the best of worms. *Rhys May Collection.*

were caretakers at Penney's Tavern and lived in a cabin at the rear. Rhys on skis and their big black dog, Jerry, in harness, made a team to fetch the mail from Casa Diablo—the first winter mail in Mammoth. A spoken command and they were off. Rhys mentions, "I sure had to be ready or he'd leave me flat!" After more than 30 years at Mammoth and now retired, they live in Oregon—fishing, hunting, and gardening.

CCC CAMPS, 1933.

The Civilian Conservation Corp (3-C Camps) was organized during the depression in 1933. For Inyo-Mono, a main camp was established above Lone Pine and a smaller camp for summer work in Mammoth, near the Hess Sawmill site. Foremen appointed by the Forest Service in charge of work groups were: Bill Reed, Lester Parent, Bud Corporon, Ed Humphrey, Chris Christensen and Art Provience. Road and trail work, cleanup and enlarging campgrounds, fire duty, and the beginning of the Ranger Station in New Mammoth were important projects. A permanent camp spot for foremen and their families was chosen back in the pines, near the Sawmill Ditch and Shady Rest Camp. Frames with floors were scattered here and there. In spring when the snow was gone there was a great flurry of moving in. We became quite expert at fitting tents on frames and setting up the wood stoves. Come fall, it was sometimes a race with the weather, as the chore of removing and drying wet tents was not a choice one. Everything had to be stored at the Forest Service warehouse across the creek, as we wintered in Lone Pine.

NEIGHBORS NORTH AND SOUTH.

"Pard" Kennedy, a prospector and former millwright, was one of the first to camp at Convict Lake. Fishermen began following the tracks through the sagebrush, and soon a Mr. Raymer established Raymer's Camp. Tent houses, boats on the lake, bait and tackle, and fishing holes on the creek—these were added attractions for eager fishermen. A new owner, Bill Garner and wife, built a lodge and cabins and began a pack camp.

RAYMER'S CAMP AT CONVICT LAKE, A FISHING CAMP. Note the tent houses scattered at the edge of the aspen grove. *H. W. Mendenhall Photo.*

 ANDREW THOMSON, WHO HAD HOMESTEADED IN THE 1860s, built a fishing camp on the Owens River in Long Valley. During his later years he wintered in Bishop, but in spring he would hitch up his horses and hie away to the camp. *Carrie (Thomson) Wonacott Collection.*

Believing strongly in the conservation of fish, Bill became widely known as a protector of newly stocked lakes in the high country. His baggy bib-overall, flannel-shirted figure, topped by a slouchy felt hat, was long a familiar sight in Mammoth.

Andrew Thomson, a great-uncle of Carrie (Thomson) Wonacott of Bishop, homesteaded land in the 1860s near the head of the Owens River in Long Valley. He later built a fishing camp that was popular many years. In 1907 Thomson sold to Fred Alpers, a cattleman in Inyo. Alpers and his sons herded their cattle to the Long Valley ranch for summers until the family moved its large herd west of the Sierra near Marysville. Later one of the sons, Bill Alpers, took over the Mono property. He and wife Alice and family for many years have operated the fishing resort known as "Alpers Owens River Ranch."

Another resort on the Owens River, farther east, was owned by Frank Arcularius. The business was managed by the Bill Garners prior to their move to Convict Lake. Then in the 1930s the guest cabins, store, and lodge came under the management of Frank's daughter Genevieve and husband, Newie Clement.

In July 1927, Clarence Wilson obtained the first permit to build and operate Crestview Lodge, in the forest opposite the State Highway Yards on Highway 395 about nine miles north of Mammoth Junction. The lodge included small, attractive cabins, supplies for tourists and fishermen, a dining room, bar, and dance floor. An unusual bartender was one Chick Reiner, a dedicated collector of butterflies from all over the world. His glass cases of brilliant, delicate butterflies covered the walls of the dance floor; it is said he later displayed them at Casa Diablo and McGee Creek Lodge. During the building of the DWP Tunnel, some families lived at Crestview and children went to a little red schoolhouse nearby. The teacher was Mrs. Lois Eikie, her husband one of the tunnel workers. These bits of Crestview history are from the Zischanks, who lived at the State Yards during 1937–38 while Max worked for the Highway Department.

CROWLEY LAKE RESORT, BISHOP, CALIFORNIA, RTE. 3 — OPEN ALL YEAR
FISHING — HUNTING — SKIING

☞ NYLE AND RUTH SMITH STARTED CROWLEY LAKE RESORT ABOUT 1947, after being in the boat-rental and guide business at Mammoth since 1921. During their years at Mammoth they wintered at Lake George.

Karl and Dorrance Keough of McGee Creek Lodge were known for their hospitality. In the late '30s skiing was just beginning here and there, maybe a rope tow, maybe not. People from outside became interested and joined the locals for some thrilling meets. The Eastern Sierra Ski Club operated a lift on McGee Mountain for a time, and the events were usually followed by evenings at the lodge, ending with singing and dancing. In 1934 the Keoughs hosted an Old Timers Surprise Dinner and Dance Party. The names of those forty-five old-timers of Inyo and Mono arouse memories of many good times!

"Happy Jack" Partridge and wife Helen and family had a small store, a gas pump, and cabins for rent on old Highway 395, above Little Round Valley. He always greeted people with a wide smile, hence the nickname. Jack recalls, "I was Supervisor in Mono for seven years and put in 25 years on the Hot Creek School Board." They are now retired in a home they built above the old road.

In about 1916 Tom Yerby bought from Hans Lof the property on Rock Creek where he and wife built a store. Through the years he added a gas station, guest cabins, then a hotel and a garage—all known as Tom's Place. In the early years Rock Creek was a stage stop on the route from Bishop to Mammoth and points north. A large meadow nearby was a stopover for the great cattle herds heading for summer graze. Hans Lof was well known as the man with a hook in place of one hand. He once cut down a tall tree, trimmed it, and donated it as the first flagpole in Bishop. It stood many years at the center of Main and West Line Streets.

Emmet Hayden, a summer cabin-owner at Mammoth, produced a map covering the fishing area from Paradise Camp to Lee Vining titled "Fishermen's Paradise of Mono County." It shows Lake Crowley, elevation 6800 feet, which was dedicated on October 24, 1941. It was a brisk autumn day. The aspens flaunted their bright colors and big, puffy white clouds floated about the high peaks. A crowd of more than 600 people gathered to witness the naming of the storage reservoir in memory of our beloved "Padre of the Desert." Father John J. Crowley, who passed away March 17, 1940, loved our mountains, valleys, and desert. His labors brought about better understanding between Inyo-Mono and the great city to the south. A quote from "Lest We Forget" by Curley Fletcher expressed our feelings: "A great man who matched our mountains and desert. He passed this way."

1248-THE MINARETS, MTS. RITTER AND BANNER, REDS MEADOWS AREA.

☝ VIEW WEST FROM MINARET SUMMIT. *Stephen Willard Photo.*

OUR GYPSY YEARS.

These "gypsy years" were good years even though there were many chores: toting water from the nearby ditch for drinking, bathing, and wash day; snow from the Summit and ice from deep down in the Earthquake Fault for a homemade ice box; and always the wood box to fill. On the bright side were the close friendships, outdoor life, campfire gatherings with games and dancing on the grass, Fourth of July picnics, and visits to the Hot Creek swimming hole.

The weekly entertainment at Shady Rest Camp was most enjoyable. Sybil Summers hosted one of special interest when she brought a group of Paiute Indians to dance before a large crowd seated outdoors around a big campfire. The tribal dances, the guttural chanting, the soft accompaniment of tomtom, and the flickering firelight were a combination hard to resist. Soon an extra figure was noted, one who knew the steps well. Our Ranger, Doug, was right in there, grinning widely. His wife, Ada, smiled and mentioned how much he loved to join in. Sybil displayed many of her choice Indian baskets and described their use, ending a most enjoyable evening of authentic local lore.

Early fall, after Jack Frost had painted bright red, yellow and orange hues among the green pines, was the time to gather the plump, ruby red, wild currant fruit. Across the narrows of Twin Lakes a little bridge led to pretty campgrounds. To the left of the road there was a large growth of currant bushes. Soon, the spicy wild fragrance of big pots of juice

STARKWEATHER CABIN, MINARET SUMMIT. "Starky" was a prospector. *Howard Jones Coll.*

simmering on the back of the wood stove filled our tent home. Making many sparkling glasses of jelly became a custom each fall.

We often traveled the old road leading from Minaret Summit down to the San Joaquin River. It was full of thrills—rough, narrow, with deep chuckholes, and a series of bumpy, so-steep switchbacks (about five in all) that were a challenge to any driver. If we didn't come into the short turns just right, it meant backing for another try! Before coming to the switchbacks the road skirted a pretty mountain meadow where wildflowers of bright colors flourished. A little stream of purest water that circled through the meadow was a delight. This road from the Summit down to the San Joaquin was built in 1926. Before then, the Minaret Mine across the canyon had to depend on mules to pack their ore out to the Summit, then the end of the road.

A mile or so below the Summit, a narrow road turned right to end at Agnew Meadow. For long years an original cabin stood in the meadow, the home of Tom Agnew who worked his mine nearby. The meadow was headquarters for the pack train managed by young Charlie Summers and family. There was a campground for hardier travelers. After negotiating the switchbacks on down the mountain, there was a parking spot and a sign, "Starky Lake." A short walk disclosed a spot of beauty. Around the shores of a small lake grew mountain azaleas whose pure white blossoms filled the air with fragrance. It was a good lake to fish in early years. Other bright flowers, tiger lily, and columbine grew in deep shade along the little outlet stream.

The banks of the river offered many spots for picnics. Fish were quickly cleaned and placed in skillet, while coffee brewed over wood coals. Just up-river was a garden of giant delphiniums, blossoms matching the blue sky. Mammoth had beautiful wildflowers, but here they grew in luxuriant abundance. We might drive on to Reds Meadow, hike to the Devils Postpile or Rainbow Falls, or stop at Pond Lily Lake. All was virgin country of pumice flats, meadows, and forest below tall mountains.

The return trip was usually accomplished in good order, although there were those switchbacks to keep in mind. We tackled them with a little prayer, "Let there be no frightened driver stalled on a short turn and, more important, no truckload of hay heading down to Archie Mahan's Pack Camp!" It was good to pull up over the Summit and return to camp.

 Our Village In The 1930s—We Called It Just <u>Mammoth</u>. This meadow area became known as Old Mammoth only after the village moved to the highway in 1937 and named itself "New Mammoth."

Far left, the Standard Service Station, boasting two visible gas pumps. The next building was, in turn, Navajo Johnson's Trading Post, Mammoth Liquor Store, and Mammoth Saloon. Far right, Lutz Grocery, which succeeded Summers Store in 1933. Left of Lutz, the Sierra Cafe, which in the 1930s served as the village gathering place—for meetings, dances, and even for the first Catholic services in Old Mammoth. Left of the cafe, alone in

the meadow, stands the only reminder of Mammoth Camp—the great rock fireplace. Half hidden in the aspen trees at the far end of the road, just as it swings to the left, is the old Wildasinn cabin. (Also belonging to our village, but out of this photo, were Penney's Bakery, the Mammoth Garage, and Forest Service headquarters—all down the road near the Mammoth Creek bridge.)

On today's Old Mammoth Road, if you align yourself with the landmarks, you can easily find the very spot, within a few feet, where Willard took this photograph in the 1930s. *Stephen Willard Photo.*

Found in Guseman Garage 1937

TELEPHONE CALLS

Bishop Central	───
Mammoth Garage	── ── ── ── ──
Convict Resort	── ─── ──
Crystal Crag	── ── ───
Casa Diablo Store	─── ──
C C C Camp	── ───
T.Cushion	── ── ── ── ── ──
Wildyrie	── ── ── ──
Hot Creek	── ── ── ──
Mammoth Store	─── ── ──
Tamarack Lodge	── ── ──
Pine Cliff	─── ── ─── ──
Ranger Station	── ─── ─── ──
Mc Cuffin	███████ ██ ████████
Rock Creek Inn	─── ─── ── ──
Hess Sawmill	─── ── ── ──
Standard Oil	── ─── ───
Tom Yerby	── ──
Mc Gee Creek	── ── ─── ───
Hot Creek Ponds	── ── ─── ── ──

OUR VILLAGE IN THE 1930s. A list of our neighbors and their telephone rings.

☝ **THE TRADING POST, AFTER NAVAJO RELOCATED IN OUR VILLAGE FROM CASA DIABLO.** Left to right: Sam and Lilas Griffith, owner Navajo Johnson, John Lutz, Laura Lutz, and Bud Lutz. *Laura (Keough) Lutz Collection.*

☝ **THE SIERRA CAFE IN OLD MAMMOTH,** where a wedding was held September 18, 1941. The bride and groom came from New York to settle in Mammoth. Seated: Marie Meckel and son, Daisy Patton, Kenzie Davidson, Mardelle Parent, Florence Nicoll. Standing: Ranger Fred Meckel, George Patton, Marg Humphrey, Everle Reed, the wedding party of six with Father Maginnis, and last, Sybil Summers. *Tex Cushion Collection.*

🖐 **MAJESTIC JEFFREY PINE IN OLD MAMMOTH.** According to Shirley Barker it was known as the Indian Tree, once a gathering place for Indians from Inyo, Mono, and Yosemite where they camped and traded. Many artifacts were found nearby. Tex Cushion's Winter Patrol Cabin was just east of the tree. The cabin and garage showing in back of the tree belong to Rhys Jones, of the pioneer John Jones family of Round Valley. Photo taken in 1931. *Marianne Huntsinger Collection.*

✒️ **FOREST SERVICE HEADQUARTERS IN OLD MAMMOTH,** on Mammoth Creek just above the bridge. It was customary to fly the flag on a tall pole. Upstream, among the willows along the creek, were several private cabins. *U. S. F. S. Collection.*

☞ **Fred S. Brooks,** born in Round Valley in 1885 and storekeeper for the Summers in Old Mammoth from 1917 to 1934. He remembers traveling to the Mammoth area with his grandfather, when he was but a boy. He is pictured with Mammoth's first gasoline dispenser, a five-gallon can with a spout. Fred contributed generously to our knowledge of early Mammoth days.

☞ **The Big Wheels That Long Stood In Front Of Crestview Lodge On Highway 395.** Note also the set of solid wooden wheels. The lodge and cabins were razed in 1977. *Both photographs by Adele Reed.*

☞ HISTORIC MAMMOTH CREEK FORD, the crossing for stages and wagons during the mining days, before there were any bridges. The ford is upstream from today's bridge. During the 1920s, although there was a bridge, the ford was used as a short cut to camping sites and to Camp High Sierra.

We are looking south across the creek. On this side of the creek, just off the photo on the left, were the remains of the Wildasinn sawmill. On the far side of the creek, the two buildings on the left are Mammoth Liquor Store and the Sierra Cafe. Left of them, just off the photo, were Lutz Grocery and the Standard Station. The Wildasinn Hotel and the Summers Hotel had burned by the time this photograph was taken, leaving ten or so cabins, most of them built by Charlie Summers.

In the cabins pictured toward the right lived: Lloyd and Sybil Summers, Charles Jr. and Altha Summers, Lee and Esther Summers, John and Laura Lutz. Also Cinto, a Mexican who made wonderful tamales; and Jens Ness, who wore colorful handmade sweaters, mitts, and socks from his homeland. *Tex Cushion Collection.*

PART V.

BEGINNINGS OF NEW MAMMOTH, 1937.

The beginnings of Old Mammoth are hazy, but there is no doubt at all that the life of the small village in the meadow ended abruptly with completion of a modern highway to Mammoth in 1937. Branching off from Highway 395 near Casa Diablo, it follows a totally different route into Mammoth, north of the old road, and then swings up into the lakes basin in long, gradual curves. The village, to survive, literally picked itself up and relocated astride the new highway, near the junction of the Old Mammoth Road and Highway 203.

he completion of Highway 203 in 1937 signaled the beginning of many, many changes. For businesses, moving from Old Mammoth was imperative, for the new highway by-passed the meadow entirely. Our village in the meadow was soon but a memory, with fat cattle roaming where once stood the Wildasinn Hotel and Mammoth Camp. The broad meadow was fenced, under the new ownership of Frank Arcularius. By 1938, the little community we called "New Mammoth" consisted of the following: the Standard Service Station, managed by George and Daisy Patton, an ice house, Lutz Store, the Post Office, Penney's Tavern, Reed's Mammoth Garage, the new Forest Service Ranger Station, plus housing for Ranger Doug Robinson and Assistant Lester Parent. Tex continued his Winter Patrol in Old Mammoth. How proud everyone was of the new and larger buildings, sheltered under tall pines. New Mammoth was a wondrous area of natural beauty.

PENNEY'S TAVERN.

When departure from Old Mammoth became a "must," the Penneys decided to build the first hostelry in New Mammoth, Penney's Tavern. By 1938 Frank Penney was busily completing a porch that provided a front entrance. Their big lobby was destined to be the community center for a number of years. The tavern stood near the corner of the new highway and the Old Mammoth Road. It was two-story with several rental rooms, and housekeeping cabins nearby. Norah Bob continued her baking, and her homemade ravioli were a flavorsome addition to her delicious dinners. Bob will be best remembered for her big picture hats (she always dressed in her best manner for any event, even to shopping in town), for her dry wit and homespun wisdom, for her poetry. The sound of her typewriter was heard in the wee small hours.

During the winter of '40 and '41, Lloyd Nicoll managed the Tavern and also the ski lift below Lookout on lower Mammoth Mountain. After

he returned from service in the Sea Bees, the Nicolls built and operated the Mammoth Lumber and Supply on the new highway above the Post Office. Frank and Bob sold the Tavern after World War II and retired to Bishop. It changed hands several times, managed in turn by Bill Treglown of June Lake, Dean Crow, Smoke Backe, Harnsbarger & Foss, and Wilma and Dick Agee. The Agees added to the bar and enlarged the dining room by including the side porch.

THE NEW MAMMOTH GARAGE.

In spring 1938, midst melting snowbanks just across from Frank and Bob's place, Bill Reed was fast completing his garage and service station. He had purchased the old garage by the creek and also moved the original Guseman cabin and set it up in back of the new garage. There was great activity—grubbing sagebrush, leveling raw land, the sound of saw and hammer. Going into business was an exciting challenge, plus a lot of hard work! Also, sadly, it meant the end of the freedom of earlier tenting years.

THE SEASONS:
SUMMER TOURISTS, FALL, WINTERING IN.

The busy summer season began with the arrival of cabin-owners, lake-resort owners (when the roads were open), and fishermen. Next, when schools were out, came long lines of tourists, their cars loaded with family and camping gear. Sometimes in tow was a luggage trailer and often a tear-drop trailer. House-trailers were a thing of the future! Summertime flew by on swift wings. Long and late hours of work ended in early fall when the tourists and deer hunters headed for home. We could relax and feel free for awhile. As Frank Penney once remarked after a particularly hectic season, "By God! I can't look another tourist in the face. Bob, you'll have to take charge, I'm heading out on a prospecting trip!"

✒ **THE TAVERN,** built by Frank and Norah "Bob" Penney. *Frank Penney Collection.*

✒ **ADELE REED AND FRIENDS,** in "dusters" (garage coats), off for a day of touring and visiting in their 1931 Packard. Time for fun after a hectic summer. Left to right: Vi May, sporting a Carmen-Miranda-style hat trimmed with golden aspen leaves; Daisy Patton; Adele at the wheel. *Bill Reed Photo.*

The golden days of early fall with a zip in the air, the blue haze of Indian summer, and the red and yellow aspens outlining waterways was a lovely time. A time of cutting and hauling winter wood, a picnic or two, duck hunting on little Casa Diablo Lake, or hunting ducks and geese and fishing down on the Owens River (no Crowley Reservoir yet). And the annual venison barbecue at the Tavern—a big event. Everyone entered in. The menfolk took turns keeping the pit barbecue fires going all night. The ladies helped Bob with huge bowls of salad, pots of beans, and many loaves of garlic bread. Tables and seats set up outdoors served the people from up and down. The Penneys were great hosts.

Winter, "shut-in time," usually began with a heavy snow sometime after the first of November, but sometimes earlier, catching everyone unaware! Winter meant long, quiet, peaceful days after the rush of summer. At times blizzards raged outdoors; at other times, the calm stillness of snow country. Snow brings unbelievable beauty to mountain country—frosted magical scenes, story-book beauty. It coats trees with fluffy white trim that melts into Christmas icicles hanging from the tip of each branch. The ever-welcome noise of the snow-go or snowplow opening our road in from Highway 395 carried through storm or quiet. Roy (Pop) Wells and crew—Chuck Kispert, Pete Maron, Bill Gish—took particular care to open entrance driveways of each business.

Tex's dog teams could be heard barking joyfully as they left the Patrol Station in Old Mammoth all the way to the Tavern, come mail time. It was our custom in late afternoon to gather in front of the big fireplace at the Tavern, visiting with friends and neighbors while waiting for the mail. For a time the mail was brought up from a box near Highway 395 by Rhys May and his sled dog; then in a hit-or-miss fashion by anyone coming in. A petition to Congress, signed by all the business people in 1941, brought delivery of mail all the way to the Tavern in winter, six days a week instead of three. Clarence Sipes, driver of the truck, made it to Penney's if the road was open and then continued on his route to Lee Vining.

THE NEW POST OFFICE.

Lloyd Summers and son Lee moved a small cabin from their pack camp near Lake Mary to a location on the south side of the highway and installed the set of mail boxes from the Lutz store in Old Mammoth. The

 Mammoth Garage, with the boss, Bill Reed, waiting on a customer. *Adele Reed Photo.*

 Rhys May Showing His 28-Inch Loch Leven To Frank Penney. *Frasher Collection, Pomona Public Library.*

Post Office was kept open from May 1st to November 1st, Sybil Summers continuing as Postmistress, driving down and back each day from the pack camp. She was known as the Smiling Postmistress, a faithful worker, come rain, sleet or snow. One day in late October we received a call for our tow truck. On the way down that morning, Sybil had hit an icy spot and her car skidded off the road. It turned over a couple of times and came to rest in an upright position. Sybil crawled out, made it up to the road, and hailed a ride to Mammoth. Though bruised and upset, she soon began sorting mail. What a lucky person she was, as we found a large, heavy meat-grinder in the back seat of her car. In 1948 the Post Office was moved across Highway 203, near its present location, Sybil continuing until retirement.

LUTZ GENERAL STORE.

In 1939 John and Laura Lutz made the move from Old Mammoth to a fine, large store in New Mammoth on the north side of Highway 203 just above the Standard Station. They managed the business for many years. Their ad on a map, produced by the Hayden Map Company in 1941, read:

> LUTZ GROCERY, Pioneer store of Mammoth Lakes. Vegetables, meats, fresh milk—light hardware, fishing tackle, camp supplies. We specialize in complete orders for your packtrip. Telephone and telegraph service. Season, May 1st to Oct. 1st. Open daily 6 A.M. to 8:30 P.M.—J. E. Lutz, Prop.

ICE HOUSES.

In 1937 Jo and Jim Wallace built a large ice house fronting on Old Mammoth Road near the Mammoth Garage. They cut and hauled their ice from Twin Lakes. They also sold hardware and lumber. Several seasons later they sold to George and Daisy "Babe" Patton, who were managing the Standard Station. The Pattons converted to an ice-making plant, not dependent on the whims of Mother Nature. Stan Hosner took over the business for a few years, and the building eventually became a clubhouse.

S. P. Keough and John Lutz, with the help of Lloyd Nicoll, built the K. and L. Ice Company in the spring of 1946 on the north side of the highway. Services included lockers, quick freezing, fish packed and shipped, deer storage, etc. The building was demolished in 1965 and replaced by a building housing the Inyo-Mono Bank (later Security Pacific Bank) and the present Post Office.

THE NEW RANGER STATION, 1938.

In later years when we attended the dedication of the new Forest Service Visitor Center at Mammoth, memories came flashing back to another day, another era, another dedication. Looking across the huge gathering of people we thought of the spring of 1938 when the Forest Service was building their new ranger station and office at the junction of Highway 203 and the Old Mammoth Road, just across from Reed's Garage and Penney's Tavern. The floor was completed when Ranger Doug Robinson came by one fine day with a twinkle in his eyes and asked, "How about helping us break in that new floor with a dance next Saturday evening, spread the word, will you?" Great activity prevailed on Saturday—the floor waxed, the tavern piano hauled over and set up in a corner, lights strung about in the trees, powered by the trusty Kohler plant. Dancing began at dusk with different ones taking turns at the piano, accompanied by guitar or banjo. Rose Boothe, wife of Forest Supervisor Roy Boothe, tuned up her fiddle for the quadrilles. The changes were called by either Roy Boothe or Bill Reed, who danced as they called. The square dances were the most popular, with a lively schottische, two step, polka and a waltz now and then filling in a happy evening.

When it came time in 1941 for Doug to retire as Ranger of the Mammoth District, luckily it was late fall after the outsiders had all departed; all of Doug's friends could attend the party held in his honor at Nan and Max's Long Valley Resort. Winter people from up and down, Forest Service personnel, relatives and friends from Bishop gathered for the big event. More than seventy people enjoyed a delicious potluck dinner. Lloyd Summers presented their gift, a slide projector, to Doug. He was an ardent photographer of desert and mountain scenery; Mrs. Doug had brought his slides and a screen, making an evening enjoyed by all.

☞ FOREST SERVICE RANGER DOUG
ROBINSON, right, with assistants Dick
"Blackie" Hollock and Les Parent sitting
on the steps of the new Ranger Station,
1937. *Les Parent Collection.*

✎ RETIREMENT PARTY FOR RANGER DOUG ROBINSON, November 17, 1941. Left to right: Sybil
Rogers, Susie Rowan, Art Kniefelkamp, Doug Rowan, Dick Rogers, Doug Robinson, Cece
Thorington, Tom Hughes, Tex Cushion, Glady Kispert, "Pop" Wells. *G. A. Packard Collection.*

THE PENGUIN CAFE.

In 1941 Dick and Sybil Rogers purchased a lot from the Summers property
on the highway near the Post Office. Dick and local carpenters Doc
Spencer, Lynn Phelps, and Elmer Cannon began building their Penguin
Cafe. On September 4, a huge crowd attended their grand opening—
nearly 150 "first nighters." Their cafe had the first soda fountain in
Mammoth, and they also specialized in evening dinners. Dick was a chef
by profession and presided in the kitchen. Sybil tended the fountain,

served short orders and the dinners with help from local girls in the summer. She mentioned one day, "We are so happy to be at the end of the road in winter for the benefit of skiers beginning to come in."

The Penguin Cafe was often used after business hours for social gatherings and for meetings of the Mammoth Mountain Ski Club. The Rogers operated the Cafe until 1959 when Roy and Eunice Crandall bought and named it "The Barbeque Hut," then just "Crandalls." New owners George and Voncile Cloudas in 1964 enlarged and re-named it "The Village Inn." After the Colwells, father and son, purchased it and rebuilt in 1969 the spacious building of today, they changed the name to "Village Center Mall." Today Pea Soup Anderson's sign marks the site.

HADDAWAY MANUFACTURING COMPANY.

John and Barbara Haddaway moved to Mammoth from Hollywood in 1947, renting and converting two of the Arcularius cabins on the hillside above the Pelton wheel. Their Haddaway Manufacturing Company produced an unusual type of patented air pump with tuned vibrator. In July

☞ **PENGUIN CAFE AND SODA FOUNTAIN,** south side of Highway 203. *Roy Crandall Collection.*

[[139]]

RUTH SMITH AND NANCY ZISCHANK, at the Crestview Easter Egg Hunt the day after the play. Several members of the cast came in their costumes, as Nancy did. *Nan Zischank Collection.*

☞ **POSTER BY BARBARA HADDAWAY,** for "The Champion of Her Sex." The play, starring Nancy Zischank and presented by the Mammoth Mountain Ski Club in April, 1949, at the Tavern, brought down the house. *Barbara Haddaway Collection.*

☞ **THE CAST POSING FOR PICTURES.** Left to right: Glady Kispert, Narca Cooper, Florence Nicoll, Frankie Stevenson, Dorothy Spaethe, Pat Weller, May McCoy, Nan Zischank. *Nan Zischank Collection.*

'56 they moved their business into a new building at the end of Chateau Road. Barbara made beautiful color posters for our plays and other events.

COMPANIONSHIP AND ENTERTAINMENT.

Close companionship and dependence on each other prevailed in those winters of the late '30s and '40s. Much of the time we were isolated, for the main highway needed all the men and the limited equipment. Opening our road was of secondary importance. There were about two dozen people, give or take a few, including the caretakers at the lakes and one mine. Between storms, we enjoyed parties and dances at the Tavern or at Casa Diablo.

We also put on our own plays. Since Olive Barker of Manahu Lodge had talent and had been trained at Pasadena's Little Theatre, she directed the one-act plays that were so popular at Penney's Tavern and later at the Hot Creek Grade School Auditorium. Usually one big event marked the end of winter. In full costume—homemade, make-do type—the play that brought down the house was titled "Shot-Gun Wedding," starring Violet May and directed by Ollie. After many weeks of rehearsing, accompanied by much hilarity, the big night arrived. A small platform with a makeshift curtain served as stage. Most of Mammoth's winter population took part, in front of a packed house! The audience came all the way from Bridgeport and Bishop. After the floor was cleared, we danced to the music of Sage McKinney and Sons and Bill Nestell into the late hours. In 1949 another play, titled "Champion of Her Sex" and starring Nan Zischank, played to a crowded house at the Tavern.

SPRING IN OUR MOUNTAINS.

Of the four seasons experienced in our mountain country, spring was the most enjoyable to us, perhaps because we could walk outdoors without having to don "snow garb." There was the feel of good earth underfoot and no slippery ice. The bright warm days, the fragrance of budding shrubbery and sagebrush—everything seemed cleansed and fresh. Of special interest was the deer migration on the lower slopes of Laurel Mountain. It was a tremendous sight! It looked as if there were thousands of deer, moving slowly towards the security of the back country and

 THE LAKES BASIN IN SPRING, Mammoth Crest forming the skyline. *Stephen Willard Photo.*

browsing on the brush as they went along. The whole mountainside seemed in motion! Jumping in their stiff-legged fashion over snow banks and high rocks, nothing stopped their forward trek!

It was our privilege to view another of nature's spectacular sights while on a towing job near Benton Crossing. Early one spring on a cold, frosty morning we were heading home with the stalled car in tow, never expecting to come across the incredible, wild spectacle of the sagehen dance! On a grassy slope above the road north of Whitmore Tubs, dozens of the puffed-up birds strutted and milled about in a glory of fan-like feathers! Old-timers called it Pow-wow. This annual gathering, taking place at a pre-designated spot in early spring, is the beginning of the mating season. After several days of "dancing," the pairs mate and go on their way. We had heard of the "dance" several times, and on this early morning a wish did come true.

 LUTZ GROCERY (MAMMOTH STORE) IN LATE SPRING, north side of Highway 203 just east of the new Post Office, lower photo opposite. The only general store in New Mammoth for years. *Laura (Keough) Lutz Collection.*

THE STANDARD STATION, managed by George and Daisy Patton, east of Lutz Store. Daisy, "Babe," ready for a ride. *Patton Collection.*

☝ **THE MAMMOTH LAKES POST OFFICE UNTIL 1948,** Sybil Summers, Postmistress. Lloyd Summers moved the cabin from his Pack Camp down to the south side of Highway 203 near the Penguin Cafe. *Harry Prier Collection.*

☝ **THE ICE HOUSE,** built by Sabert Keough and John Lutz. It specialized in quick freezing, packing and shipping fish, and deer storage. Note the new Post Office, across the highway from the one pictured above. Today's Post Office and a bank now occupy this site. *Laura (Keough) Lutz Collection.*

SKI at ...
Mammoth

Mammoth Mountain

Where you can ski longer every year. Where the first snow falls ... and the last snow melts!

Penneys' Tavern
MAMMOTH LAKES, CALIF.

In The Inyo . Mono High Sierra

Mammoth In Winter

State Highway Snow Removal Equipment Keeps
the Road Open to Mammoth

•

For Your Winter Comfort

PENNEY'S TAVERN

44 Miles North of Bishop on U. S. 395

offers

Hotel Rooms at $2.50 Single and $3.50 Double; Modern Housekeeping Cabins. $1.50 per Person.

Cabins—Single Day, per Couple at $3.50, Completely furnished.

Dormitory—$1.00 per Person Without Bedding, $1.50 per Person with Bedding Furnished.

WEEKLY RATES ON APPLICATION

•

Every Cabin and Room with Oil Heat!

•

Come to the land of winter, where the sun shines down
on the Switzerland of America!

CAFE ... BAR ... STORE

Phone, Write or Telegraph

PENNEY'S TAVERN

LLOYD NICOLLS, Manager 1941

Mammoth Lakes, Calif.

Independent-Progress Press

THE TAVERN, 1942. *Frasher Collection, Pomona Public Library.*

POP WELLS AND CREW OPENING THE ROAD TO TWIN LAKES, 1940. *Harry Prier Collection.*

☝ **Our Home Sweet Home,** 1938–1948, in back of the Mammoth Garage. Our daughter's dog, Pal.

✍ **Old Mammoth Road,** 1941, looking south near Reed's Garage and Penney's Tavern, just off Highway 203.

✍ **The New Mammoth Garage,** winter 1941, across the Old Mammoth Road from Penney's Tavern. Built in 1937–'38 by Bill Reed, helped by Doc Spencer, Lynn Phelps, and Elmer Cannon. We were snowed in for two weeks over Christmas. We had turkey and a Christmas tree but no outside mail! *Adele Reed Photos.*

PART VI.

BEGINNINGS
OF SKIING.

Adele's story of Old Mammoth ends with this chapter, for in 1948 she and Bill sold their garage and moved to Bishop. She makes no attempt to chronicle the vast changes that have occurred since then.
"That's for someone else to do," she says.
"I am writing what I know and what
I saw, people's own stories."

he sport of skiing has zoomed far, far beyond our wildest imaginings in the 1940s. Beginning in the '30s with portable rope or cable tows set up on any likely slopes that were accessible, skiing now plays a major role in the economy of Mammoth Lakes. In those early years McGee Mountain became *the* place! Many of the first events were held here and training schools for beginners were operated by Dave McCoy, Hans Georg and others. The Eastern Sierra Ski Club (ESSC), with headquarters in Bishop, began to promote competition skiing. George Deibert, Bob Crosby, Bob Kelso and others gave time and effort. Ruthie Janes of the ESSC was a great worker toward school skiing. Hans had come from St. Moritz, Switzerland, where he had been an instructor. In later years he operated his own lift and ski school on the lower, eastern slope of Mammoth Mountain. In his stone cabin nearby, he wrote two books on skiing, *Reverse Shoulder Technique* and *Modern Ski Systems*.

To the north, the Mono Ski Club organized, using lifts at June Lake. The Inyo-Mono Association (Bob Brown, secretary) was busily engaged in the overall promotion of winter sports. Their slogan was, "The road is always open to the snow country!"

MAMMOTH MOUNTAIN SKI CLUB.

The year 1941 was actually the beginning of a concentrated effort by Mammoth residents to find a solution to many problems. Badly needed were the following: an organization to promote winter business; a community hall; daily mail service; and snow removal from the highway as far as Twin Lakes bridge. Many meetings finally brought forth on March 1, 1941, an organization of 123 charter members, both local and outsiders. It named itself Mammoth Mountain Ski Club and combined with a Winter Sports Association. First president was Lloyd Nicoll with these other

 McGee Mountain, The Place To Ski In The 1930s. The base of the rope tow was just off old Highway 395, half a mile north of McGee Creek. During the '30s and early '40s, most races and events were held here because McGee had the only dependable, fixed tow of any length and, being adjacent to the highway, it was easily accessible by car. *Harry Prier Collection.*

Skiing In The 1930s, Rope Tow Housing, base of McGee Mountain. Across the road, the Pete Steffen Fox Farm. Note the absence of Crowley Lake reservoir; the dam was not yet built. *Tex Cushion Collection.*

Dave McCoy, during McGee Ski School days. *Nan Zischank Collection.*

officers: R. C. Rogers, vice-president; Sybil Rogers, secretary-treasurer; and directors Tex Cushion, William Reed, James Wallace, Nyle Smith, Max Zischank, Elmer Cannon, and Harry Prier. The club joined the Inyo-Mono Association and the California State Ski Association. A duplicating machine was purchased and bulletins were mailed to agencies in Southern California. Club emblems were made up for members and the local skiers participated in races and events.

CHAMPIONSHIP RACES 1941.

The thrilling races of the Inyo-Mono Championship Meet were held at the club's lift on McGee Mountain on March 16, 1941. Close competition in the downhill and the slalom between Augie Hess, Mono Ski Club, and Dave McCoy, ESSC, placed Augie as the new champion by a slight margin. These two placed first and second in the combined results for the meet. Others that placed were Frank Stevens 3rd, ESSC; Irving Dow 4th, ESSC; Stan Hess 5th, Mono SC; Claude James 6th, ESSC; Vernon Holland 7th, ESSC; Cliff Banta 8th, Mono SC; Larry Hess 9th, Mono SC; and 10th place, Dick Morrison ESSC. In the women's combined, Nan Zischank 1st, Mammoth SC; Eunice Yongue 2nd, Mono SC; Helen Tibbals 3rd, ESSC; Barbara James 4th, ESSC; and Jackie Dow, ESSC,

⊲NANCY ZISCHANK, winner of the Inyo-Mono Women's Championship in 1941 and 1942, with the George Deibert Perpetual Trophy. Other winners were: Ruth Ewing, 1937; Lona Anderson, 1938; Marie Meckel, 1939; Roma Carriere, 1940. *Nan Zischank Collection.*

placed 5th. The Eastern Sierra Ski Club received praise for their very well-conducted meet. The crowd gathered at McGee Creek Lodge where a buffet dinner was hosted by Dorrance Keough. Master of ceremonies was Dr. Scott of Bishop. After the presentation of awards and trophies, singing and dancing ended the enjoyable day.

Another race (and one of the most sensational) was sponsored by the Mono Ski Club in 1941 at June Lake, assisted by the Mammoth Mountain and Pasadena Clubs. It was the "Flying Skis" 5-mile Carson Peak run. Hazardous, but most thrilling, this race began at an elevation of 11,000 feet with a drop of nearly 4000 feet. The long trek to the summit took about 4½ hours; the race began at 10:30 A.M. As the skiers arrived at the top and came into view they looked like tiny ants to the watchers below. The run had been planned and laid out by top-ranking skiers from other areas and included the roughest features of several famous runs. Only two women ever attempted this race. In 1941 Clarita Heath of the Mono SC made the run in 8:40.3 to win over Nan Zischank of the Mammoth SC with 15:02. In 1942 Nan was the only woman to make this run and won the perpetual trophy, given by C. B. Harrison of the Southern California Auto Club. The Carson Peak run was at one time believed to be the longest and most difficult down-mountain course in the world. Nan attributes her skill on skis to the early teaching of Tex Cushion on the little hill back of the Winter Patrol in Old Mammoth; she also had a short period of training with Hans Georg.

COSTUME EVENTS ON SKIS.

Great preparations were underway in April for the annual costumed Easter Egg Hunt on Skis, scheduled to take place Easter Sunday morning on the lower slopes of Mammoth Mountain, using the Lloyd Nicoll ski lift. Tex Cushion originated the event in 1938 at McGee Mountain, assisted by his wife Ruth and Nan and Max Zischank. It became a colorful, popular event. Tex presented the idea to the Mammoth Mountain Ski Club; they adopted it as their yearly fun event. The club appointed Tex to manage the 1941 affair, with the following committees: refreshments, Jim Wallace; races, Tex Cushion; egg planting, Tex Cushion, Dutch Spaethe, Russell Howard; judges, Nyle Smith, Lynn Phelps, Elmer Cannon, John

☞PROGRAM FOR THE CHAMPIONSHIP SKI MEET AT MCGEE MOUNTAIN, March 3, 1940. In the late 1930s the Eastern Sierra Ski Club began to promote competitive skiing.

During these early years most tows, unlike the fixed tow at McGee, were small, portable affairs, put together by anyone who liked to tinker and who could find an old Ford or Chevy gasoline motor, a rope, and some pulleys. A dozen different slopes between Whitney Portal and Conway Summit sported tows at one time or another. A "crowd" might consist of 15 people; an all-day ticket might cost two dollars. Rigging up a tow was less of a problem than finding a suitable slope that one could drive to. State Highway crews kept 395 open all winter, but almost no side roads into the mountains were cleared of snow. Hence most people located their tows somewhere along Highway 395, following the snow to wherever the slopes were good.

FOURTH ANNUAL
Inyo-Mono Championship

Ski Meet

Auspices Eastern
Sierra Ski Club

McGee Mountain
March 3rd, 1940

RACES

Sunday, March 3, 1940

10:00 A. M.—Women's Giant Slalom.
10:30 A. M.—Men's Giant Slalom
1:00 P. M.—Women's Slalom
2:00 P. M.—Men's Slalom

ENTRANTS

Clifford Banta .... Mono Ski Club
H. C. Blaver .... Mono Ski Club
Leo Castagno .... Eastern Sierra Ski Club
Marshal Carriere .... Eastern Sierra Ski Club
Robert Conroy .... Eastern Sierra Ski Club
Tex Cushion .... Eastern Sierra Ski Club
Irving Dow .... Eastern Sierra Ski Club
Carl Grebe .... Eastern Sierra Ski Club
Lloyd Goodale .... Eastern Sierra Ski Club
August Hess .... Mono Ski Club
Stanley Hess .... Mono Ski Club
Larry Hess .... Mono Ski Club
C. M. Houston .... Eastern Sierra Ski Club
Claude James .... Eastern Sierra Ski Club
Bob Janes .... Eastern Sierra Ski Club
Chester Janes .... Eastern Sierra Ski Club
Dean Kiner .... Eastern Sierra Ski Club
Dave McCoy .... Eastern Sierra Ski Club
Fred Meckel .... Eastern Sierra Ski Club
Joe Miller .... Eastern Sierra Ski Club
Paul Patten .... Eastern Sierra Ski Club
Jack Pelose .... Mono Ski Club

RACE COMMITTEE

Chester Janes—Chairman
Dave McCoy, Claude James, Fred Meckel, George Farrel

Timers—J. A. Schwab, H. A. Van Loon, Pat Coons.
Starter—Ed. Parker.
Course Setter—Courtland Hill.
Recorders—Lorenzo Dow, Wm. Whorff.
Judges of the Finish—J. A. Schwab, H. A. Van Loon, Pat Coons.

ENTRANTS

Dr. C. L. Scott .... Eastern Sierra Ski Club
Eugene Shaffer .... Eastern Sierra Ski Club
Nyle G. Smith .... Eastern Sierra Ski Club
Frank Stevens .... Eastern Sierra Ski Club
Gerald Yongue .... Mono Ski Club
Richard C. Rogers .... Unattached

WOMEN

Roma Carriere .... Eastern Sierra Ski Club
Madeline Castagno .... Eastern Sierra Ski Club
Jackie Dow .... Eastern Sierra Ski Club
Ruth Ewing .... Eastern Sierra Ski Club
Barbara James .... Eastern Sierra Ski Club
Opal Miller .... Eastern Sierra Ski Club
Marie Meckel .... Eastern Sierra Ski Club
Eunice Yongue .... Mono Ski Club
Nan Zischank .... Eastern Sierra Ski Club

☜ HANS GEORG, who came in 1938 from St. Moritz, Switzerland, one of the first ski instructors at McGee Mountain. Later he operated his own lift and ski school on the lower slopes of Mammoth Mountain's east face, living in his stone cabin nearby. *Laura (Keough) Lutz Collection.*

☞ CARL GREBE, NAN ZISCHANK, AND TEX CUSHION, racing at McGee Mountain, 1941. *Harry Prier Collection.*

Lutz; tabulator, Sybil Rogers; prizes, Adele Reed and Florence Nicoll; egg dying, Ruth Cushion (thirty dozen eggs!). Eggs were hidden at the base of 150 slalom poles. "One pole will hold the 'jackpot' of a dozen eggs, and a few will be blanks!"

The show began at 11 A.M. with an opening address, followed by formation skiing through single and double slalom flags. Next was the thrilling barrel-stave race. The barrel staves could not exceed 36 inches in length and no ski poles allowed. Much time and labor had gone into preparing the staves—shaping, smoothing, and waxing. This was a straight "schuss" from the top of the run to the gate, entrants sometimes finishing on hands and knees! These races were followed by the costume parade. Homer Harris and his 10-foot skis was notable. (He was the six-foot-plus singing cowboy entertainer at Tom's Place.) The parade featured all sorts of costumes, from a court jester (Frankie Stevens of Bishop) to the professor-who-forgot-his-pants (Otto Krause, ski instructor at McGee Mountain). The final event was the Easter Egg Hunt on Skis. Since participants were not allowed to carry any sort of container for the eggs, the results were quite hilarious. Fun and mix-ups ended in a final dash down-mountain for inspection, timing, and counting eggs. Augie Hess, Mono Club, placed first for the men with 18 eggs; Marie Meckel, ESSC, women's first with 11 eggs; Don Banta, Mono Club, first in children's division (by finding the "jackpot" of 12 eggs). Dick Rogers, Mammoth Ski Club, made the spectacular time of 12½ seconds to win the barrel-stave race. Cliff Banta and Augie Hess of the Mono Club came in second and third. A closing address by "Slim" Mabery of June Lake ended the first big affair held on Mammoth Mountain slopes. Several hundred people enjoyed the fine day.

VISION OF THE FUTURE.

Roy Boothe, Supervisor of the Inyo National Forest, was asked to assume leadership in promoting a get-together of all rope-tow operators and club representatives. It was held at McGee Creek Lodge April 4, 1941. The meeting brought forth good plans for more housing, larger lifts, and snow removal. One paragraph from Roy's letter of invitation points up clearly that he was a man of great foresight:

☞ ROY BOOTHE, PHOTOGRAPHED ON PALISADE GLACIER. Roy was Supervisor of the Inyo National Forest, with headquarters in Bishop. Roy and his staff deserve much credit for working with the people of Mammoth to promote skiing and development. *Frasher Photo, Pomona Public Library; Rose Boothe Collection.*

Please come prepared to contribute constructive ideas and co-operative effort into putting Inyo-Mono winter sports on a business basis. And in a position to grow in popularity with other winter sports areas of California, eventually assuming its rank among the best of them.

He knew his forest country well. His predictions of over forty years ago have come true and in a big way!

DAVE MCCOY:
MAN OF VISION, MAN OF ACTION.

The name Dave McCoy (and the McCoy Family) is synonymous with Mammoth Mountain and with skiing. Dave's enthusiasm for the two has never wavered. Since his first rope tow at Grays Meadow west of Independence prior to 1936 and then his progression to Bishop, McGee

Mountain, and Mammoth Mountain, his advance has been steady, forward and determined, despite the ups and downs. Among the "downs," we recall fractures and broken bones during his racing days; short winters when he was depending on plenty of the white miracle that covers bare ski slopes; or an over-abundance of snow that covered buildings, lifts and roads, bringing everything to a standstill. Whimsical, unpredictable winters!

Dave and his wife Roma (Carriere) were active in the original Mammoth Mountain Ski Club and Winter Sports Association and in the first ski events. Dave also managed the McGee Ski School. In winters he moved portable tows here and there following the snow. In 1941 he set up his first rope tow on Mammoth Mountain. According to the newspaper:

> Over 250 skiers visited Mammoth Mt. over the Thanksgiving weekend. The portable tow, operated by Dave McCoy, was run overtime to accommodate the enthusiastic crowd! *Inyo Register, November 20, 1941.*

In December Dave had to move out as snow closed the road and no roads were cleared then to the mountain. Later, skiers made it to the mountain on the Army-surplus Weasels that Dave acquired. The Weasels were the first equipment used on the mountain; they played a great part in getting skiers up and then back. This in-and-out business continued until 1947 when McCoy, on the promise of open roads, built his first small building on Mammoth Mountain. Eventually he built his first ski lift at the foot of the broad, beautiful north face—a skier's paradise.

Through the years Dave has been ably sided by his wife, Roma. She is a very skilled skier in her own right. They raised six children, four boys and two girls, in the family tradition—skiers all. The McCoy family has earned recognition in many ways, both national and international. Dave's name was included many years ago in the National Hall of Fame. Asked recently if he ever dreamed that his ski land would become a "Kingdom of Its Own" he just grinned and replied, "No, definitely! But it's been a lot of fun!" And thus it continues.

☞ **THREE OF THE McCOY FAMILY:** Roma, Dave, and their son Gary. *Dave McCoy Collection.*

COSTUME PHOTOS TAKEN DURING THE 1941 EVENT. Above left, Homer Harris got one scrambled. Above right, "I did have two! Where did I put them?" Both photos, G. A. *Packard Collection.* Lower right, the McCoys made a winning pair. *Nan Zischank Collection.* Opposite page, the costume parade included Homer Harris on ten-foot skis and the absent-minded professor who forgot his pants. G. A. *Packard Collection.*

☞THE EASTER EGG HUNT ON SKIS, which originated in 1938, grew into a popular, hilarious annual costume event. Poster by Barbara Haddaway for the 1949 hunt, held at the Deadman area above Crestview. Participants were not allowed to have any sort of container to carry their eggs; the photos show how some people solved this problem. *Barbara Haddaway Collection.*

✎ PROGRAM FOR THE 1941 EASTER EGG HUNT.

Mammoth Mt. Easter Egg Hunt on Skis

Sunday, April 13, 1941

11:00 A. M.
Opening Address

11:15 A. M.
Formation skiing through single and double slalom flags by skiers in costume.

12:00 NOON
BARREL STAVE RACE

12:45 P. M.
HOMER HARRIS and his 10-foot skis, and COSTUME PARADE.

1:15 P. M.
EASTER EGG HUNT.

2:00 P. M.
Closing Address.

Costume Easter Egg Hunt

Mammoth Mt. Ski Club's
TWELFTH ANNUAL EVENT

COSTUME PRIZES
FOR CHILDREN AND GROWNUPS

SKI RACES WITH PRIZES
BARREL STAVE RACE

EVERYBODY COME
COME IN COSTUME

Easter Sunday from 12:30 on.

 MORE EASTER EGG HUNT PHOTOS. Events were held wherever the snow was best, this time above Crestview. Prizes were ski clothing or equipment. Left, Roma and Dave McCoy. Right, Doc Scott, an enthusiastic skier.

BARREL STAVE RACE, the finish line, 1941 Easter Egg Hunt on Skis. Does anybody have more fun than skiers? *Nan Zischank Collection.*

☞ Ballot For The Combined Mammoth Mountain Ski Club And Mammoth Winter Sports Association. The groups organized on March 1, 1941, with 123 charter members. They sponsored races and events and promoted winter business.

BALLOT

for candidates for officers of Mammoth Winter Sports Association and Mammoth Mountain Ski Club for 1942

PRESIDENT (Vote for one)
TEX CUSHION—Winter Patrol Station; member Board of Directors 1941; 1941 delegate California State Ski Convention. ☐

MAX ZINSCHANK—Long Valley Resort; member Board of Directors 1941; 1941 delegate California State Ski Convention. ☐

☐

VICE PRESIDENT (Vote for one)
LYNDEN PHELPS—Shang-ra-la Ski Hut, Twin Lakes. ☐
JOHN LUTZ—Mammoth Grocery. ☐

☐

SECRETARY-TREASURER (Vote for one)
ADELE REED—Mammoth Garage, chairman Refreshment Committee 1941. ☐

NAN ZISCHANK—Long Valley Resort; winner women's division Inyo-Mono Ski Meet. ☐

☐

ASSOCIATION BOARD OF DIRECTORS (Vote for five)
LLOYD NICOLL—President 1941; Mammoth Mountain Ski Lift 1941. ☐

RICHARD C. ROGERS—Penguin Cafe; Vice President 1941; Barrel stave race champion, Easter Egg Hunt, 1941. ☐

ALLEN PERCELL—Tamarack Lodge winter season 1941-42. ☐
WILLIAM REED—Mammoth Garage; Board of Directors 1941 ☐
RUTH CUSHION—Winter Patrol Station. ☐
NYLE SMITH—Smith's Ski Hut, Lake George; Mammoth Mountain Ski Lift 1942. ☐

FRANK PENNEY—Penney's Tavern. ☐

☐

☐

☐

☐

☐

SKI CLUB BOARD OF DIRECTORS (Vote for three).
A. G. ANDREWS—4235 E. 2d st., Long Beach; sportsman; Mammoth booster. ☐

JACK TRUITT—4307½ So. Olive st., Los Angeles; sportsman; Mammoth booster. ☐

LEE SUMMERS—Casa Diablo; Mammoth Pack Train. ☐
GEORGE DEIBERT—Bishop Drug Co.; sportsman, skier. ☐
JERRY PACKARD—Mammoth Garage; club photographer 1941.

FLORENCE NICOLL—Valentine's Camp; Mammoth booster; skier. ☐

☐

☐

☐

Signature of voter ....

Present Address ....

Mail Ballot immediately to Mammoth Mountain Ski Club Nominating Committee, Mammoth Lakes, via. Bishop, Cal.

Election and installation of officers December 12. Ballots must be in by before that time.

BALLOTS BY COURTESY PENGUIN CAFE

🖐 **SKIING IN THE 1940s.** The broad slopes of Mammoth Mountain's famous north face, before any lifts were built. Mammoth Mountain has everything a skier dreams of—open slopes, wonderfully variable terrain, a long ski season, and many days of clear, sunny weather. However, a major problem in the '40s was just getting to the mountain's north slope. That problem was not solved permanently until the mid-'50s, with construction of a new road. In the early '40s, from the road end, wherever that might be, you walked in or skied in or hoped someone had managed to borrow a Caterpillar to pull you in. *Stephen Willard Photo.*

📄 **VIEW WEST FROM MAMMOTH MOUNTAIN**—the Ritter Range with the Minarets, Mount Ritter, and Banner Peak. Photo by Charles Kassler III, *Dave McCoy Collection.*

📄 **SKIING IN THE 1940s WITH ARMY-SURPLUS WEASELS.** World War II years were quiet years at Mammoth, but after the war more people than ever became interested in skiing and Dave McCoy solved the transportation problem temporarily by acquiring some Army-surplus Weasels. The Weasels hauled people back and forth, from their cars to his tows at the base of the mountain. One Weasel story concerns two of them, hauling people down one evening, when something went wrong with one of them. A very long rope, fastened to the back of the good Weasel, hauled a total of 106 skiers on that run. *Dave McCoy Collection.*

MAMMOTH TAVERN
MAMMOTH LAKES, CALIFORNIA

🖐 **BEFORE CHAIR LIFTS, RIDING UPHILL ON NUMBER TWO ROPE TOW TO GRAVY CHUTE,** Mammoth Mountain. You gripped the wet rope with your hands or with a "gripper," a nutcracker-like gadget attached to a rope around your waist. It was hard work either way, requiring very strong hands. In the distance far left, San Joaquin Ridge. *Dave McCoy Collection.*

📖 **BEFORE CHAIR LIFTS, RIDING UPHILL BEHIND A TUCKER SNOW CAT.** The two ticket offices and the building behind them were the beginning of today's Mammoth Mountain ski complex. *Dave McCoy Collection.*

📖 **MAMMOTH TAVERN,** formerly Penney's, the only place to stay overnight in Mammoth for a good number of years. When it was full, skiers often drove to Bishop over 40 miles away. *Laura Lambert Collection.*

⬳Skiing In The 1950s, Number One Chair Lift, Mammoth Mountain. Major obstacles to Mammoth Mountain's becoming a ski center were solved in the 1950s. A graded all-weather road was built to the base of the north slope, assurances were given that the road would be cleared in winter, and Dave McCoy built his first chair lift in 1955. *Dave McCoy Collection.*

✍Skiing In The 1950s. Left, the first passengers to ride Number One Chair, Roma McCoy and Jill Kinmont. *Dave McCoy Collection.* Right, Gloria Redmon and Jill Kinmont. *Nan Zischank Collection.*

☝Skiing In The 1950s. The Lodge With Number One Chair in the distance, left of center, north slope of Mammoth Mountain. Mark Zumstein, now of Bishop, has contributed much information about these early ski photos. He was active in the Mammoth Mountain Ski Patrol beginning in 1947 and continuing until only a few years ago. *Dave McCoy Collection.*

Stephen Willard Photo.

TODAY MAMMOTH IS A FAMOUS RESORT. New faces, new businesses— today's Mammoth is a far cry from the old mining camps, from the village in the meadow, from the small town on the new highway. Now the upswing of progress absorbs much of the natural, primeval beauty of this country. Yet the grandeur of the surrounding mountains is just as inspiring as in the early years. They are still "mountains to look up to," God's country.

NOTES ON THE PHOTOGRAPHS.

[BY GENNY SMITH, EDITOR].

Many, many days of research have gone into identifying the photographs in this book. However, you will notice that few of them carry a photographer's credit line and fewer still are dated. Most of the photos come from old albums, old trunks, or from boxes that have been passed from one generation to the next—with no record of who took them or when. Anyone having information on any of these photographs is urged to write the editor: P.O. Box 1060, Mammoth Lakes, CA 93546. We will be very grateful.

Following are a few notes on the Adele Reed Collection and on the four professional photographers whose works are included: A. A. Forbes, Burton Frasher, Harry W. Mendenhall, and Stephen H. Willard.

THE ADELE REED COLLECTION.

Unless noted otherwise, all photographs in this book are from Adele Reed's collection of historic photographs. She has been collecting photographs, souvenirs, letters, stories, memories, old bottles, and hundreds of other items of historical interest ever since she and Bill moved to the eastern Sierra in 1927. Her knowledge of eastern Sierra history led to her first book, *Old Bottles and Ghost Towns*, first published in 1961 and having eleven printings. Her other titles are: *Charm, History and Heritage*, 1965; *Bottle Talk*, 1966; *Swing Your Partner*, 1968; *Mammoth Lakes Memories*, 1971; and *We Dug Those Dumps*, 1974. She continues to write articles on local history for the Bishop newspaper, *The Inyo Register*. Some of her Old Mammoth photos were first published in *Mammoth Lakes Memories*. This book, *Old Mammoth*, is based on *Mammoth Lakes Memories*; the text has been revised and expanded and many photographs, maps, and illustrations have been added. We are grateful to Adele's many friends from Old Mammoth days who have generously loaned their photographs for publication in *Old Mammoth.*

A. A. Forbes [1862–1921].

Most of his early years, Andrew A. Forbes lived with his family in Iowa or Kansas. We know few details of his years after he left home, other than that he took photographs in Oklahoma in 1889, became an itinerant photographer, wandered westward, and in 1898 set up a studio in Santa Ana, California. Around 1902 he moved to Bishop, where he opened "Forbes Studio." In 1909 he married Mary R. Prutzman, who became the studio's business manager. Until 1916, when they moved to southern California, A. A. Forbes photographed extensively along the eastern Sierra. (This information comes from Nancy Peterson Walter, Research Associate, Los Angeles County Museum of Natural History, who has done much research on Forbes and his photographs.)

Burton Frasher [1888–1955].

Burton Frasher was a box maker, following the fresh fruit harvest from California's oranges to Washington's apples until 1914 when he decided to become a commercial photographer. He opened his first store in La Verne and in 1921 moved to Pomona. Fishing and photographing in the High Sierra led to making postcards of local scenes at the request of a few resort owners. The business mushroomed into Frashers Fotos, which supplied millions of black-and-white view postcards throughout the southwest. In 1965 Burton Frasher Jr. donated the collection of 60,000 glass plate and film negatives to the Pomona Public Library.

Harry W. Mendenhall [died 1952].

We know nothing of Harry Mendenhall's early life. The first record we have of his being at Mammoth is his signature in the Wildasinn Hotel Register on July 24, 1908, giving Lida, Nevada (a mining camp) as his residence. The first record of his being in Big Pine is his registration for the primary election in Big Pine precinct, in 1910. Just when he began his career as a photographer we don't know, but we do know that he married Edith M. Calkins in 1921 and that they established their Camera Art Shop in Big Pine, 15 miles south of Bishop. After his death in 1952, Edith continued operating the store and selling his postcards until her own death in 1976. We are very fortunate that Edith gave her friend, Adele, many of Harry's prints and permission to publish them.

Stephen H. Willard (1894—1966).

Stephen Willard set up his first photo studios in Idyllwild and in Palm Springs in southern California. He married his wife, Beatrice, in 1921. Looking for a location for a summer studio, they discovered Mammoth Lakes. They built their studio in 1923 and opened the following summer. For many years they operated their Palm Springs studio during the winter and their Mammoth studio during the summer. In later years they wintered at their ranch in the Alabama Hills near Lone Pine. After his death, Beatrice continued the studio until her own death in 1977. We are most fortunate that Beatrice gave her friend, Adele, many of Steve's prints and permission to publish them in her books.

NOTES ON THE TEXT.

[BY GENNY SMITH, EDITOR].

PLACE NAMES AND MAPS. We supply notes on only a few of the place names—when they are obscure, when today's names are different from those used in Old Mammoth days, or when they are unusually interesting. Most place names mentioned in the text are currently used and can be located on maps of the Mammoth Lakes area. All California road maps show the major towns and roads. The best single, detailed map of the area is the Forest Visitors Map, 1972, Inyo National Forest, 30 × 40 inches, ½ mile = 1 inch (available from ranger stations or the Forest Supervisor, Inyo National Forest, Bishop, CA 93514). Maps with even more detail are the USGS topographic maps, 15-minute series, 1 mile = 1 inch (purchase by mail from Topographic Division, USGS, Federal Center, Denver, CO 80225). Quadrangles for the area the text describes are: Bishop, Casa Diablo Mountain, Cowtrack Mountain, Devils Postpile, Glass Mountain, Mono Craters, Mt. Morrison, Mt. Tom, White Mountain Peak.

Part I.

[PAGE 1]. MAMMOTH LAKES. The village of Mammoth Lakes, elevation 7850 feet, lies just east of the Sierra Nevada crest in Mono County, California. By air it lies 180 miles due east of San Francisco and 30 miles west of the California-Nevada State Line. By road it is about 160 miles south of Reno and about 300 miles north of Los Angeles. It is three miles west of Highway 395.

[PAGE 3]. BISHOP. Elevation 4147 feet, 40 miles south of Mammoth Lakes. Largest city in Inyo and Mono counties. In early days known as Bishop Creek.

[PAGE 3]. OLD YANEY PLACE. Corner of Highway 6 and Wye Road.

[PAGE 4]. **U. S. Forest Service.** Most land around Mammoth is federal land managed by the U. S. Forest Service as the Inyo National Forest. Forest Supervisor's headquarters, Bishop; Mammoth District Ranger's office, Mammoth Lakes. The Sierra National Forest adjoins the Inyo on the west. Today's Ranger Station is half a mile east of the "new ranger station" built in 1938, p. 137.

[PAGE 4]. **Pine Crows.** Clark's nutcrackers; also known as Whiskey Jacks.

[PAGE 4]. **Wild Canaries.** Warblers migrate through the area in May, probably Wilson's warbler.

Part II.

[PAGE 13]. **Mineral Hill.** Locally called Red or Gold Mountain. Rises steeply over 1500 feet above the mining camps. On its slopes, tunnels, dumps, trenches, corner markers, and rusted metal are still noticeable today.

[PAGE 14]. **Arrastra.** A crude drag-stone mill for pulverizing ores, in which heavy stones are dragged over pieces of ore. Often powered by a burro, mule, or (as this one) a water wheel.

[PAGE 14]. **Pelton Wheel.** Though always called locally the "old Pelton Wheel," this is a Knight wheel, the difference between the two being the design of the cups. *See* Mammoth Mining Company Mill, below.

[PAGE 14]. **Mammoth Mining Company Mill.** Reporting on the property in 1888, Mining Engineer H. A. Whiting described it this way: "In the summer of 1878, a twenty-stamp mill was put up by the Mammoth Company, to which twenty stamps were added the following spring. The stamps weighed nine hundred pounds each. The mill was driven by a six-foot Knight wheel, under an effective head of about one hundred and seventy-five feet. Provision had also been made to drive the machinery by steam; but no occasion seems to have arisen for the application of that power." *Eighth Annual Report of the State Mineralogist*, California State Mining Bureau, 1888, p. 375.

[PAGE 15]. **Eastern California Museum, Independence.** Independence, the County seat of Inyo County, is about 85 miles south of Mammoth Lakes.

[PAGE 21]. **Redd's Lake.** Now called Sotcher Lake; also known as Pond Lily Lake. The lake and Reds Meadow are named for Red Sotcher (or Satcher)—a large red-bearded man who came here in 1879 herding sheep. The story is that Sotcher began raising vegetables in the meadow when he realized there was a market for fresh produce at the Mammoth mining camps just over the hill.

[PAGE 21]. **MONUMENTAL ROCK.** Now called Mammoth Rock. See photo p. 46.

[PAGE 23]. **DEADMAN.** Another story about the name of Deadman Creek and Deadman Summit is in W. A. Chalfant's *Gold, Guns, and Ghost Towns,* Chapter 3, Stanford University Press, 1947. It concerns a man who, while searching for the Lost Cement Mine, killed his partner and took his money. The dead partner's body was found in this creek.

Part III.

To trace the routes described in this chapter, see these USGS topographic maps published in the early 1900s, *not* the recent 15-minute series: Bishop, 1913; Mt. Goddard, 1912; Mt. Morrison, 1914; Mt. Lyell, 1901; Bridgeport, 1911; Hawthorne, 1909. These are out of print but can be found in libraries with good map collections.

[PAGE 29]. **CARSON AND MOHAVE.** Carson City and Mojave, mentioned in the ads, were all-important railroad connections. Carson, 150 miles from Mammoth, was the headquarters of the Virginia & Truckee Railroad, which connected at Reno with the transcontinental Central Pacific Railroad. Mojave, 220 miles of desert south of Mammoth, was a main yard on the Southern Pacific Railroad from San Francisco. Until 1883, when the Carson & Colorado narrow-gauge railroad was built from Mound House near Carson to Owens Valley, Carson and Mojave were the railroad connections for all the eastern Sierra mining camps.

[PAGE 29]. **CERRO GORDO FREIGHTING COMPANY.** A large enterprise—12 stations and 80 teams of 16 mules, each team pulling three huge wagons—formed by M. W. Belshaw and Victor Beaudry (the tycoons of Cerro Gordo) with teamster Remi Nadeau to haul silver-lead bullion from the Cerro Gordo mines in the Inyo Mountains to Los Angeles. Cerro Gordo shut down in 1879, just as Mammoth City was booming.

[PAGE 30]. **BODIE.** A large and long-lived gold and silver mining camp north of Mono Lake. Boom days, 1877–1881; peak population, 8,000.

[PAGE 30]. **ROUTE TO BODIE.** Deadman's Station was probably near Deadman Creek; King's Ranch, later known as Cain Ranch, was near the junction to Grant Lake; the Goat Ranch, later the Scanavino Ranch, was on the north side of Mono Lake near the mouth of Cottonwood Canyon.

[PAGE 30]. **ROUTES FROM BISHOP CREEK.** All routes had to climb the steep rise from Round Valley (about 4,000 feet) to Long Valley (close to 7,000 feet). *See* Sherwin Grade, below.

[PAGE 30]. **SHERWIN GRADE OR SHERWIN HILL.** The steep 3,000-foot rise between Round Valley and Long Valley.

[PAGE 30]. **SHERWIN SUMMIT.** The Summit, Grade, Creek, and Meadow were all named for Jim (J. L. C.) Sherwin.

[PAGE 30]. **MONO MILLS.** A large sawmill in the Jeffrey pine forest east of the Mono Craters and south of Mono Lake, built to supply lumber to Bodie.

[PAGE 32]. **WICHA CABIN AND SPRING.** Spelled Witcher Meadow and Creek on today's maps.

[PAGE 32]. **BENTON HOT SPRINGS.** Also known as Old Benton, a silver mining camp about three miles west of Benton (or Benton Station), which is on Highway 6.

[PAGE 32]. **AURORA.** A boom town from 1859 to 1869, ten miles east of Bodie in Nevada. Gold and silver.

[PAGE 32]. **ARCULARIUS RANCH.** There were two ranches. The one on the Owens River is still a fishing camp, the other in the Old Mammoth Meadows is now a condo development.

[PAGE 34]. **FRESNO.** A town west of the Sierra Nevada, in the San Joaquin Valley.

[PAGE 34]. **OLD FRENCH TRAIL.** Built by J. S. French. Sometimes called the Mammoth Trail. Even today the 20 miles of trail from Reds Meadow to Clover Meadow can be followed easily. West of Clover Meadow extensive logging and road building have erased much of the old trail.

[PAGE 34]. **FRESNO FLATS.** Today known as Oakhurst.

[PAGE 34]. **MEDARA.** Madera, a San Joaquin Valley town 20 miles north of Fresno.

[PAGE 36]. **CLOVER MEADOW.** Near the Granite Creek roadhead on the Sierra's west slope, 20 miles by trail from Reds Meadow.

Part IV.

[PAGE 43]. **CHARLES F. WILDASINN.** The earliest records we have found of Charlie Wildasinn's arrival in Mammoth are two Tax Deeds dated May 12, 1891, in the Mono County Courthouse, which record his purchase of 40 acres and 120 acres, both parcels sold for delinquent taxes. Other records document numerous purchases through 1901, some from individuals and others from the tax collector. In 1897 he received a patent from the General Land Office for 160 acres. The

Owens Valley Herald carries this ad in numerous issues, beginning June 28, 1909, "I am prepared to take boarders at the Casa del Saro Hotel at Mineral Park. Unexcelled table. C. F. Wildasinn." This item appears in the July 16 issue. "C. F. Wildasinn, proprietor of the Casa del Saro hotel at Mineral Park, was in Bishop Monday. His resort is proving more popular this year than ever before."

[PAGE 50]. SIERRA COUNTY. A county in northeastern California.

[PAGE 51]. MAMMOTH LAKES POST OFFICE. *Mammoth Post Office* was the name first selected. When it was discovered that a Mammoth Post Office already existed in northern California, *Lakes* was added. Mammoth Lakes it has been ever since.

[PAGE 57]. TOWNSEND GRAVE. For the story of the Townsend grave, see the book *A Child Went Forth* by Helen MacKnight Doyle, Gotham House, 1934. Out of print, but available in libraries.

[PAGE 59]. BIG WHEELS. Also called Michigan Wheels.

[PAGE 64]. PIUGA. These caterpillars are one of the stages in the two-year life cycle of the Pandora moth. They feed on needles of the Jeffrey pine. Epidemics occur at intervals of about 20 to 30 years and may continue for six to eight years. A recent outbreak began in May 1979 in the Jeffrey pine forest between Dry Creek and Deadman Summit. According to local Paiutes and other residents, the numbers in 1979 were the greatest they have ever seen.

[PAGE 66]. VALENTINE CAMP. In 1972 Carol (Mrs. Edward R.) Valentine donated 136 acres of the Valentine property to the University of California, which manages it as the Valentine Eastern Sierra Reserve.

[PAGE 73]. TOURIST BUSINESS BEGINNING. New roads built for automobiles (as well as faster autos) were a major factor contributing to the increasing tourist travel to Mammoth. The first bond issue to acquire and construct a California State Highway system was approved in 1910. The 220 miles between Mojave and Bridgeport were included in the first highway plan; the initial project was grading and oiling the worst part of the entire wagon road (Sherwin Hill). Almost a thousand people celebrated the completion of the Sherwin Hill project in 1916 with a barbecue in Rock Creek Canyon. Something to celebrate indeed, travel time from Bishop to Mammoth was reduced to 2½ hours. Bit by bit, automobile travel became quicker and easier. By 1931 paved highway stretched all the way from Los Angeles to Bishop.

[PAGE 73]. LAKES BASIN. The Lakes Basin is four miles southwest of Mammoth and a thousand feet higher. In it lie twelve sizable lakes and several more smaller ones, all draining into Mammoth Creek. See photo p. 143.

[PAGE 75]. **MAMMOTH CREST.** Also, the crest of the Sierra Nevada. The steep western wall of the Lakes Basin divides the waters flowing east into the Owens River from the waters flowing west into the Middle Fork of the San Joaquin.

[PAGE 76]. **GOLDFIELD.** A large mining town in Nevada, active 1903–1940. Its mines produced gold, silver, lead, copper; estimated peak population, 20,000.

[PAGE 77]. **LAKE MARY STORE.** A block structure now replaces the old store, which burned.

[PAGE 85]. **CAMP HIGH SIERRA.** A family summer camp operated by the City of Los Angeles Department of Recreation and Parks.

[PAGE 91]. **CROWLEY LAKE.** The largest reservoir in the Los Angeles Aqueduct system. Dam completed in 1941. The meadows, now covered by water, were prime summer pasture for Owens Valley cattle.

[PAGE 94]. **SAN JOAQUIN RIVER.** Unless noted otherwise, *San Joaquin* refers to the Middle Fork of the San Joaquin, which drains the huge canyon lying between the Ritter Range and, opposite, Mammoth Crest, Mammoth Mountain, and San Joaquin Mountain.

[PAGE 96]. **MINARET SUMMIT.** Pass north of Mammoth Mountain.

[PAGE 96]. **MINARET MINE.** Minaret Mines Company operated through two winters but never hit pay dirt.

[PAGE 96]. **STARKWEATHER CABIN.** J. W. Starkweather, from Santa Maria, was a prospector who worked claims on the slopes near Minaret Summit during the 1920s. According to Art Hess, he was a small wiry man with a peculiar glint in his eye. With pick and shovel he built a narrow road to the Summit, which in the 1920s was often referrred to as Starkweather Summit. He extended his road down the west slope to his claims, where he started a tunnel.

[PAGE 97]. **CITY TUNNEL CAMP.** The Los Angeles Aqueduct construction camp, east of Highway 395 near the Aeolian Buttes, for the 11-mile-long Mono Craters Tunnel. The Mono Basin Project, including the tunnel, was completed in 1940. This tunnel sends Mono Basin waters, which would normally flow into Mono Lake, south into the Owens River system and on south to Los Angeles.

[PAGE 104]. **BENTON CROSSING.** Today's Benton Crossing is about four miles north of the old crossing, which is now covered by Crowley Lake waters.

[PAGE 106]. **HIGHWAY 395.** The major north-south highway in eastern California, which runs from the Oregon border to San Bernardino, passing through Reno and Carson City, Nevada. Between Round Valley and Mammoth, today's

4-lane highway follows a different route from "old" Highway 395. In fact, today's route is quite similar to the "Dry Road" on Fred Brooks' map, p. 31. Much of old 395 is still maintained as a secondary road: west of the present highway between McGee Creek and Tom's Place, and in Rock Creek Canyon. To trace the old route in detail, see the 15-minute topo maps mentioned on p. 180.

[PAGE 106]. CASA DIABLO. The springs dried up during the 1960s, after several geothermal wells were drilled and capped. Casa Diablo and other nearby areas may have the potential to produce electricity or steam heat. After a long quiet period, by summer 1982 Casa Diablo again has active vents, some giving off hot water, some steam.

[PAGE 119]. ROAD FROM THE SUMMIT TO THE SAN JOAQUIN RIVER. The present graded route to Agnew and Reds Meadow did not exist at this time. The road described switchbacked straight down the west slope from the Summit. This was Starkweather's old road, extended by the Minaret Mines Co. down to Pumice Flat and the San Joaquin River.

Part V.

[PAGE 129]. HIGHWAY 203. The designation of the road between Highway 395 and Mammoth has changed through the years. To avoid confusion, we call it by its present name, State Highway 203.

[PAGE 131]. PENNEY'S TAVERN. Re-named Mammoth Tavern, the building was demolished in 1969. Today's Mammoth Tavern farther down the Old Mammoth Road, resembles the old tavern in name only.

Part VI.

[PAGE 153]. MCGEE MOUNTAIN. The base of the ski tow was just off old Highway 395, half a mile north of McGee Creek. The tow ran up the northeast slope of McGee Mountain.

[PAGE 162]. MAMMOTH MOUNTAIN SNOWFALL. Sierra Nevada snowfall varies tremendously from year to year, in depth as well as in timing. Maximum snow depth, the winter of 1976–77, was 36 inches on March 3. Maximum depth the winter of '68–'69 was 227 inches on March 2. (All measurements at 9600 feet on Mammoth Mountain.) Skiable snow often arrives by Thanksgiving, but occasionally it doesn't arrive until January; then again, it may come the first week of November. Whatever the snowfall, however, Mammoth Mountain is blessed with the longest season of any Sierra ski resort.

INDEX.

[NOTE] ☞ Page numbers in italics indicate photographs and captions that have been indexed. If a photo and its caption are on opposite pages, both pages are indexed and both page numbers are in italics.

[NOTE] ☞ On pages with all photographs and no text, page numbers are not printed. To find these pages, count from the nearest text page.

[H]

Haddaway, Barbara & John, 139, *141*, *164–165*

Haddaway Mfg. Co., 139, 142

Hammarborg, Lizzie & John, 76

Hampton, Ruth, 63

Harnsbarger & Foss, 133

Harris, Homer, 160, *164*, *165*

Hayden, Emmet, 116

Heath, Clarita, 157

Hess, Arthur W. & Fred M., 59, 62

Hess, Augie, 156, 160

Hess Sawmill, 59, *61*, 62, 80, 88

High Sierra Worm Farm, 111–112

Highway 203, 79, 186; completion of, 129, 131

Highway 395, *31*, 99, 106, 107, *158*, 185; completed paving of, 184

Hollock, Dick, *138*

Home Lumber Co., 58–59

Hosner, Stan, 136

Howard, Russell, 96, 157

Huckaby, George, family, 58, 60

Hughes, Tom, *138*

Humphrey, Ed, 112

Humphrey, Marg, *123*

[I]

Ice harvest, 86–87, 88–89

Ice houses, New Mammoth, 136–137, *145*

Indians from the western Sierra, 64, *109*, *124*. *See also* Paiute Indians

Inyo-Mono Association, 153, 156

Inyo National Forest. *See* Forest Service

[J]

Jackson, Dave, *94*

Janes, Ruth (Ewing), 153, *156*

Johnson, Barney & Eddie, 77, 99

Johnson, Navajo, *108*, *123*

Jones, Rhys, *124*

[K]

Kelso, Bob, 153

Kennedy, "Pard," 113, 157

Keough, Dorrance & Karl, 116. *See also* McGee Creek Lodge

Keough, Philip P., 32

Keough, S. P., 137, *145*

King's Ranch, 29, 30, 182

Kinmont, Jill, *172*, *173*

Kispert, Glady & Chuck, 135, *138*, *140*, *141*

Kniefelcamp, Art, 85, *138*

Krause, Otto, 160

[L]

Lake Crowley dedication, 116

Lake George, 75–76

Lake Mamie, 78–79

Lake Mary, 12, 13, 14, 17, 20, 76, *77*, *102–103*, *175*

Lake Mary Store, 77, 185

Lake Mining District, 11–26; beginning of, 11–12; mining camps, 13–14; water diversions, 14; newspapers, 14–18; social life & customs, 14–18; relics of, 19–20; letters about, 20–23; ending of, 18

Lake Mining Review. *See* Newspapers

Lakes Basin, *46–47*, 72, 75, *83*, *143*, 184

Lof, Hans, 116

Logging. *See* Sawmills

Long Valley Resort, 107, 110, 137

Lost Cement Mine, 12

Lutz, Bud, *123*

Lutz Grocery: Old Mammoth, 105, *120–121*, *126–127*; New Mammoth, 136, *144*

Lutz, Laura & John, 32, 105, *123*, *126–127*, 136, 137, *145*, 160

Lundy. *See* Mill Creek Canyon

[M]

Mabery, Slim, 160

McCoy, Gary, *163*

McCoy, May, *140*, *141*

McCoy, Roma & Dave, 153, *154–155*, 156, 161–162, *163*, *164*, 166, *172–173*

McGee Creek Lodge, 116, 157, 160

McGee, Elizabeth (Gunter) & Alney and family, *52*, 56, 111

McGee, John, 36

McGee Mountain, 153, 157, 161–162; skiing on, 116, *154*, *155*, 156, *158–159*, 160, 186; ski school, *154–155*, 162

McGuffin, Alice & Don, 79, 86, 93–94

McKinney, Sage & Sons, 142

McMurphy, Pat, 4

OTHER PUBLICATIONS ON CALIFORNIA'S EASTERN SIERRA COUNTRY.
[EDITED AND PUBLISHED BY GENNY SMITH].

MAMMOTH LAKES SIERRA.

By C. Dean Rinehart, Genny Smith, Elden Vestal, Bettie Willard. Many maps and illustrations, 68 photographs, index, 192 pages. Fourth edition, 1976. Authoritative, best-selling guidebook to the superbly beautiful fifty-mile portion of the eastern Sierra slope north of Owens Valley.

DEEPEST VALLEY: GUIDE TO OWENS VALLEY, ITS ROADSIDES AND MOUNTAIN TRAILS.

By Paul Bateman, Dorothy Cragen, Mary DeDecker, Raymond Hock, E. P. Pister, Genny Smith. Companion book to *Mammoth Lakes Sierra.* Out of print. Revised edition planned for 1984.

OWENS VALLEY GROUNDWATER CONFLICT.

By Paul H. Lane and Antonio Rossmann. Maps, 28 pages, 1978. Critical issues of the Inyo County lawsuit to limit groundwater pumping for the Los Angeles Aqueduct. A reprint of the new chapters in the 1978 edition of *Deepest Valley.*

EARTHQUAKES AND YOUNG VOLCANOES ALONG THE EASTERN SIERRA NEVADA AT MAMMOTH LAKES 1980, LONE PINE 1872, INYO AND MONO CRATERS.

By C. Dean Rinehart and Ward C. Smith. Two-color; illustrated with maps, diagrams, and 30 photographs; 64 pages, 1982. Relates today's events to the violent jerkings and explosions that have been shaking this eastern California region for a very long time.

[FOR PRICES AND MAIL ORDER INFORMATION WRITE]:

WILLIAM KAUFMANN, INC.
95 FIRST STREET, LOS ALTOS, CA 94022.